TEXAS
BOOMTOWNS

TEXAS
BOOMTOWNS
A HISTORY OF BLOOD AND OIL

BARTEE HAILE

THE
History
PRESS

Published by The History Press
Charleston, SC
www.historypress.net

Copyright © 2015 by Bartee Haile
All rights reserved

First published 2015

ISBN 978.1.54020.256.7

Library of Congress Control Number: 2015949873

For the thousands of Texans who risked life and limb to usher in the Age of Oil and the loved ones so many tragically left behind.

Library of Congress.

CONTENTS

ACKNOWLEDGEMENTS

The rare and remarkable photographs are what make this a special book. As the credits show, most of the truly outstanding images come from two sources: the DeGoyler Library at Southern Methodist University in Dallas and the Houston Metropolitan Research Center. This is my third collaboration with Timothy J. Ronk and Joel Draut at the HMRC, and once again, they have gone above and beyond the call of duty on my behalf. Curator of photographs Anne Peterson, plus Katie Dziminski and Terre Heydari, was a wonderful surprise. They went out of their way to assist a stranger they know only from e-mails and telephone calls. To all the above, my heartfelt appreciation.

And as always, I am deeply indebted to my wife, Gerri, whose contributions as proofreader, editor and constructive critic continue to make me a better writer.

Introduction

In 1964, the year I graduated from high school in suburban Dallas, gasoline was selling for 19.9 cents a gallon. I could fill up my Plymouth Valiant convertible for $4.00 or less, depending on how empty the tank was when I coasted into the station, and get a free glass and trading stamps. That was in the middle of what was called back in those days a "gas war."

The point of that personal anecdote from the distant past is that the fossil fuel for our internal combustion engines was so cheap we did not think about it. We pulled up to the pump, yanked the spare change from our pockets and handed it to the attendant with instructions to put in that much. Yes, a stranger pumped the gas for you!

As a native Texan, I knew, of course, that I lived in the state with more oil than any other place in the world. On long drives to West Texas, where most of my relatives lived, I saw more derricks and pump jacks than I could have counted had I chosen to pass the time that way. And I listened to older members of my extended family tell hair-raising stories of the boomtowns—Mexia, Ranger, Desdemona and Borger—that forever changed the Lone Star State.

So it could be said that this book was sixty years in the making, though I would say the last thirty-two have had the most influence because that's how long I have been writing the only statewide newspaper feature on the history of Texas. Of the 1,670 columns I have researched and written up to now, the subject of more than a few has been the gusher era and oil boomtowns. It is a popular topic with most of my readers, but there are exceptions.

INTRODUCTION

The one that comes to mind is a woman who strenuously objected to the terrible wrong I had done her hometown of Mexia. She had lived there all her life and never heard of the oil boom getting so out of hand that the governor had to declare martial law and send in the National Guard. That never happened, she insisted with righteous indignation, and concluded her letter with the demand that I stop telling such vicious lies.

I decided that the most effective answer was to mail her copies of the newspaper and magazine articles, as well as book excerpts, on which the "offensive" column was based. Once she had read and digested this material, I invited her to let me know if she still believed I made the whole thing up. Needless to say, I never heard another peep out of the poor woman, who evidently had been the unwitting victim of a "code of silence" on a sensitive subject.

I am prepared for similar letters and e-mails in response to the publication of *Texas Boomtowns: A History of Blood and Oil*. Again I will strive to show polite restraint and hopefully help open a closed mind. At the same time, I do understand why some people take so personally the public airing of dirty linen, whether it concerns kinfolk or their community. But in the end, the truth will come out like it or not.

BARTEE HAILE
AUGUST 2015

1

It All Started at Spindletop

Texas at the end of the nineteenth century was the land of cattle and cotton. Since there were no cows to punch and no cotton to pick in town, 83 percent of the 4 million Texans lived out in the country or in communities with less than 2,500 people. San Antonio, Houston, Dallas and Fort Worth, the four largest cities, in that order, had a combined population of 167,000. Texas, like the rest of the old South, was a rural state, pure and simple.

The fact that there was oil in Texas was no secret. For centuries Indian tribes had wondered what to do with the black, sticky substance that oozed from the ground and thickened into puddles. Spanish explorers who came across tar balls on the beaches in the 1500s used the gooey substance to waterproof their leather boots.

For nineteenth-century ranchers and farmers desperate for water, oil was an annoyance that got in the way and poisoned their wells. As late as 1902, W.T. Waggoner, owner of one of the biggest ranches in the Lone Star State, famously said, "I wanted water, and they got me oil. I tell you I was mad, mad clean through. We needed water for ourselves and our cattle to drink." He sang a different tune a decade later after the Electra discovery added millions to the Waggoner family fortune.

Most historians credit Lyne T. Barret with drilling the first productive oil well in Texas history near Nacogdoches in 1866, the year after the end of the Civil War. He strived to scrounge up the money and technology to make the most of the find but struck out on both counts. Reconstruction made investors skittish about risking their capital in Texas, no matter how promising the prospects, and the equipment had not been invented to efficiently pump, store and transport crude oil (often just called "crude") to market. The biggest problem was what to do with the oil once it was extracted. Locomotives and other steam-powered engines burned coal. Before the mass production of motor vehicles with internal combustion engines, the primary uses for the fossil fuel of the future was lubrication and kerosene for lamps, a limited market to be sure.

Due more to a lack of interest than a lack of effort, thirty years passed without any progress on the petroleum front in the Lone Star State. Then one day in 1897, an executive with Standard Oil opened a letter with a Corsicana, Texas postmark. It was from the top official of a town Joseph Stephen Cullinan had never heard of, and the mayor swore with the zeal of a tent evangelist that his community was sitting on top of a fortune in black gold.

Cullinan, the son of Irish immigrants, was born in Pennsylvania on New Year's Eve 1860 a short distance from the first oil well on the North American continent. The ambitious Irishman went to work for John D. Rockefeller as a twenty-two-year-old roughneck and, in a decade and a half, worked his way up to the front office at Standard Oil.

The Texas politician closed his letter with an open invitation to Cullinan to drop by and take a look whenever he had the chance. On a cross-country trip later that year, the skeptical easterner stopped at Corsicana just to satisfy his curiosity. A guided tour of the local terrain convinced the self-taught geologist that the mayor was on to something so big that he cancelled his West Coast vacation.

Moving at a speed that made the Texans' head spin, Cullinan arranged the financing for the first pipeline and refinery in state history, which he christened the J.S. Cullinan Company. The Yankee struck oil with his first round of exploratory wells, and the next thing the people of Corsicana knew was that they had a bona-fide boom on their hands. But before anyone could count his money, their patron had to figure out what to do with so much crude (two million barrels by the end of 1900), no small challenge in the horse-and-buggy era. Cullinan solved the problem, at least in part, by extolling the virtues of petroleum as locomotive fuel and a dust-settling agent for dirt roads.

IT ALL STARTED AT SPINDLETOP

Meanwhile, in the southeastern corner of the Lone Star State, Pattillo Higgins had become the laughingstock of Beaumont with his unshakeable certainty there was a sea of oil hidden under Spindletop Hill, a salt dome south of the city. With a résumé that included draftsman, inventor, artist, geologist, cartographer, engineer, naturalist and industrial designer, the fourth-grade dropout was entitled to a fair hearing. But most people were so blinded by his youthful transgressions and his dogmatic disposition that their knee-jerk reaction was to reject anything that came out of his mouth.

In his teens, Higgins was a troublemaking terror. The climax of his adolescent crime wave was a confrontation with sheriff's deputies that left one lawman dead and the seventeen-year-old with an arm so badly injured it had to be amputated. At his trial for murder, Higgins claimed he shot the deputy in self-defense, and the sympathetic jury acquitted him of all charges. Five years of raising hell as a one-armed lumberjack ended one night at a Baptist revival where the preacher persuaded him to turn his back on his evil past. "I used to put my trust in pistols," the born-again believer often said, "but now my trust is in God."

Returning to Beaumont a changed man, Higgins went into business for himself making bricks. On a visit to brick and glass factories back East, he saw the superiority of ovens that burned oil and gas. He remembered the salt dome on the edge of town that old-timers had long maintained held an unlimited supply of the same two resources. Higgins decided Spindletop was the perfect spot for an industrial center and for years could think of little else.

No men of means and influence in Beaumont wanted to have anything to do with Higgins's pipe dream. But in George W. Carroll, he finally found his financial angel. Carroll committed himself body, soul and bankroll to the Spindletop project not because he shared his controversial vision but because they were two peas in the same religious pod. The devout Baptist would come to regret his role in turning God-fearing Beaumont into a wicked boomtown and spent the rest of his life trying to repent for his sin. Twice he was a candidate on the Prohibitionist ticket, for governor in 1902 and two years later for vice president, and gave away his personal fortune to Baylor University and a host of charitable causes. Carroll died in 1935 practically penniless in a room at the Beaumont YMCA built with his money.

By 1899, Higgins had nothing but three dry holes to show for Carroll's generosity. Even more than money, which he had a flair for finding, he required an expert on salt domes with the know-how to push pipe through unstable layers of sand to the oil down below. So he launched a nationwide talent search with advertisements in newspapers, magazines and industry publications.

That was how Pattillo Higgins and Captain Anthony F. Lucas met. The Austrian-born and educated engineer answered the ad with a chapter-and-verse history of his life and career that impressed the Texan, who took pride in never being impressed by anybody, whatever their credentials.

Higgins had cast a wide net and by pure luck had hooked the foremost authority on salt domes. As superintendent for a salt-mining operation in Louisiana, Lucas had detected trace amounts of oil deep down in the dome deposits. For that reason alone, he was more open to Higgins's heretical views, though not as passionate.

Higgins had lost control of Gladys City Oil, Gas and Manufacturing, the company he founded in 1892, to the board of directors. Since he was not on speaking terms with his estranged partners, it fell to Lucas to negotiate the rights to Spindletop Hill. After cutting Higgins in for 10 percent of the profits, the naturalized citizen was ready to drill.

But like Higgins and others before him, Lucas had no answer for the sand that caused the hole to cave in every few feet. Running out of money and ideas at a depth of only 575 feet, the dejected captain called a time-out to weigh his options. With the fanatic Higgins and his own wife urging him to stick with it, Lucas sold two East Coast investors who had been instrumental in the development of the Corsicana field on the promise of Spindletop. They agreed to put up the money on one condition: Pattillo Higgins was out in the cold.

Every bit as significant as the infusion of cash was driller Curt Hamill's cure for the collapsing sand as described on the website of the Paleontological Research Institution: "Instead of pumping water down the hole to flush out the cuttings produced by the action of the drill, he used mud. This proved to help not only in retrieving the cuttings, but just as importantly, it was found that the mud stuck to the sides of the hole and kept it from caving in…mud has been used in almost every drillhole around the world ever since."

Hamill's master stroke made slow but steady progress over the next two months. With the well down to 880 feet, Captain Lucas told the crew to take the Christmas holidays off and come back to work on New Year's Day.

In good spirits and well rested after their break, the workers pushed past one thousand feet in a week. They were lowering the drill back down the hole after an equipment change on the morning of January 10, 1901, when mud mysteriously began bubbling to the surface. That had not happened before, and everyone stopped to stare at the strange sight. Seconds later, the drill pipe shot straight up out of the hole spewing mud all over the rig and the transfixed crew. Baffled by the weird antics of the well, they withdrew a safe distance to wait for the all-clear.

Five minutes passed without a sound from the Lucas One or the uneasy roughnecks. The silence was suddenly shattered by a noise stunned spectators would compare to a "cannon shot." The ear-splitting sound was the overture for a high-speed eruption of mud and natural gas that preceded the main attraction: a geyser of oil that soared 150 feet into the clear Lone Star sky.

Captain Lucas was chewing the fat with a friend in a downtown Beaumont store. The telephone rang. The owner answered and handed the receiver to the

Standing room only at a well somewhere in southeast Texas. *San Jacinto Museum, MSS0200-227, Houston Public Library, HMRC.*

visitor. "It's your wife," he casually informed him. Lucas listened in slack-jawed amazement to the wonderful news that Spindletop was indeed the real thing.

For nine days, the wild well defied every effort to contain its phenomenal flow. By Lucas's reckoning, the early rate was 100,000 barrels a day, more than all the producing oil wells in the United States put together.

The broad smile on the farmer's face said it all in this photograph from the Hull Oil Field in Liberty County. *MSS0100-0455, Houston Public Library, HMRC.*

IT ALL STARTED AT SPINDLETOP

"Buckskin Joe" Cullinan wasted no time in getting from Corsicana to Beaumont. One of the first true oilmen on the scene, he alerted his former associates at Standard Oil to the history-making discovery. Surprised by their failure to grasp the game-changing significance of Spindletop, he made up his mind that Standard Oil's loss would be his gain. To ensure his success, Cullinan built a storage tank, bought every drop of cheap crude he could lay his hands on and sat back to wait for the price to go up.

Beaumont went from a decidedly dull town of nine thousand to a full-blown boomtown of fifty thousand in six months. By the end of 1901, Spindletop was studded with two hundred closely packed wells owned and operated by one hundred separate companies. Gulf, Amoco, Humble and other charter members of "Big Oil" got their start at Spindletop.

Reckless drilling practices, as well as outright sabotage, often sent sections of the Spindletop field up in flames. During a particularly dangerous blaze, Joe Cullinan implored a district judge to grant him broad emergency powers to fight the fire. The hard-nosed oilman read the order issued by the obliging magistrate and snorted in disgust, "This is not enough!"

"What more do you need?" the judge asked. Cullinan replied, "I want the authority to kill a man if such is necessary in the discharge of my duty!" The order was promptly amended to give Buckskin Joe the power of life and death at Spindletop. When word spread that he could legally shoot troublemakers on sight, arsonists and assorted wrongdoers made themselves scarce.

In 1902, Cullinan and several oilfield cronies merged with eastern money lenders to form the Texas Company. For eleven years, the Irishman served as president of Texaco, and his relocation of the company headquarters to Houston in 1905 set the stage for the inevitable emergence of the Bayou City as the oil capital of the world.

Houston skyline in 1926 with two more tall buildings under construction. *MSS0100-1216, Houston Public Library, HMRC.*

Hugh Roy Cullen, Houston oilman and philanthropist, gave
away most of his $200 million fortune before his death in 1957.
RGD0005F3519-001, Houston Public Library, HMRC.

It was not in Pattillo Higgins's nature to sulk in the shadows over being shut
out of Spindletop. He sued Lucas and Gladys City Oil for a share of the
royalties and settled out of court for a presumably substantial amount. He
created a new company and drilled on his thirty-three-acre lease in the center of
Spindletop. But as was his lifelong inclination, he put so much of his oil income
into real estate that he did not have the liquid assets to fend off a takeover by
John Henry Kirby. Higgins sold out to the timber tycoon for $3 million, enough
to keep him on the fringes of the oil business for the next fifty years.

The oil wells at Damon Mound in Brazoria County were the last wells drilled in Texas by Captain Anthony Lucas of Spidletop fame. *34MSS0100-0023, Houston Public Library, HMRC.*

When he was not in the oilfields, Higgins was chastising the people of Beaumont on their sinful lives. Based on an unorthodox reading of the scriptures, he believed in the possibility of moral perfection, which brought him into conflict with the traditional Christian view of human beings as imperfect creatures predestined to sin. He ranted and raved against every form of public recreation and entertainment from swimming and dancing to theaters and saloons. But it was the middle-aged bachelor's adoption of teenage girls that raised the most disapproving eyebrows and resulted in accusations of hypocrisy. After marrying one of his live-in wards when she turned eighteen, Higgins spent more and more time away from Beaumont at his homes in Houston and San Antonio. It was in the Alamo City that the "Prophet of Spindletop" passed away in 1955 at the ripe old age of ninety-one.

Captain Anthony Lucas beat Higgins to the grave by thirty-four years. A quiet, dignified man who valued his privacy, he shunned the spotlight after Spindletop. Badgered by reporters, he stopped granting interviews and abandoned Beaumont the year after pulling off the feat that put his name in the history books.

Lucas worked in Mexico, Romania and Russia before returning to the Lone Star State. He drilled his last Texas well at Damon Mound in Brazoria County but did not hang around for the acclaim he deserved for opening another oilfield. The publicity-shy captain was sixty-six years old at his death in Washington, D.C., in 1921.

Horrified by the wasteful practices at Spindletop, Buckskin Joe Cullinan predicted a premature peak in production that would lead to a steep, unstoppable decline. Hoping to avoid the calamity, he lobbied for federal regulation of the infant industry and went so far as to advocate price-fixing

Since oil was considered an unlimited resource, waste was rampant in early twentieth-century oil fields. *Library of Congress.*

Downtown Beaumont circa 1925. The Spindletop bust proved to be nothing more than a bump in the road for the resilient city. *MSS0334-0839, Houston Public Library, HMRC.*

by the government. He later reverted to a conservative mindset and warned Washington to keep its bureaucratic nose out of the oil business.

For many years, Cullinan flew the Jolly Roger from the top of his office building in downtown Houston. The prominent display of the notorious skull and crossbones puzzled pedestrians and became quite

Right: The oilfield at Goose Creek on Galveston Bay before a storm blew through. *MSS0100-1205, Houston Public Library, HMRC.*

Below: The aftermath of the May 24, 1919 storm at Goose Creek oilfield southeast of Houston. *Library of Congress.*

the conversation piece. Did the buccaneer banner suggest the oil mogul saw himself as a petroleum pirate? Nothing could be farther from the truth, the New Deal critic once explained. The Jolly Roger served "as a warning to the privilege and oppression within and without the law, the latter including witch burners, fanatics and the like who fail to realize that liberty is a right and not a privilege."

During a visit to San Francisco in 1937, Cullinan was shaken from his slumber by a mild tremor. Fearing a repeat of the catastrophic quake three decades earlier, he fled his hotel room wearing only a pair of thin pajamas. Buckskin Joe caught a cold in the chilly night air but stubbornly ignored the ailment until it worsened into a bad case of pneumonia. By the time he finally sought medical attention, there was nothing doctors could do except watch him die.

His eccentricities aside, Cullinan correctly foresaw the short life expectancy of the Spindletop boom. Off to a running start of three and a half million barrels in 1901, production increased fivefold the next year to 94 percent of the Texas total. The overabundance drove the price for a barrel of oil down to an all-time low of three cents, rendering it, for all practical purposes, worthless. But the boom was finished two years later after production fell to the 1901 level of three and half million barrels.

Like rats deserting a sinking ship, thousands of recent arrivals vacated Beaumont, leaving the original inhabitants with the elbow room they sorely missed. Because it was a city of long standing, not dependent on oil for its existence, it survived the bust as it had the boom. Unlike most of the boomtowns to follow, Beaumont ended the decade with a net gain in population: twice as many residents (20,600) than it had the day Spindletop blew its top.

2

A COUNTY GONE CRAZY

After Spindletop and the series of falling-domino strikes along the Gulf coast, the Texas oil boom ran out of gas. The high expectations that kept prospectors and the public on pins and needles into the second decade of the twentieth century were brought down to earth by the failure to find the next big pool of black gold. By 1915, the Lone Star State ranked a weak fourth in petroleum production behind Oklahoma, California and, believe it or not, Kansas, and Texans had begun to ask, "Is that all there is?"

The one place not worth looking was west of Fort Worth. This widely held opinion was expressed by a wisecrack heard in every part of the state: "I'll drink all the oil in West Texas!" At the time, the quip contained a large kernel of truth that made sense to most people but not to a mining engineer by the name of William Knox Gordon, who was certain that beneath the peanut patches and cotton fields of Eastland County there was a prodigious pool of black riches just waiting to be found.

The Virginian came to Texas in 1889 with every intention of going back to the Old Dominion as soon as he finished surveying the route for a new railroad. But the Texas Pacific Coal Company based in Thurber made Gordon an offer he could not refuse, and a quarter of a century later, he had worked his way up to general superintendent of the biggest mining operation in the state.

Gordon relaxed by taking long horseback rides and came to know the sparsely settled landscape like the back of his hand. Due to his basic grasp of geology, he came to know something else. There was oil under

Roarin' Ranger provides the background for this shot of a portion of the oilfield. *Library of Congress.*

the tiny town of Ranger and most of Eastland County. He pestered Edgar Marston, president of Texas Pacific, until he broke down and sent a geologist to investigate Gordon's hunch. When the respected rock-hound found nothing to support the superintendent's claim, he begged the big boss to send another geologist and another after that. In spite of the three strikes, Gordon would not admit he was "out" and traveled to New York City at his own expense to lobby the company president in person. More impressed by the employee's stick-to-itiveness than his hare-brained idea, Marston told him to "go ahead" all the while expecting nothing to come of it.

Determined not to spend a dime more than necessary out of TP's piggy bank, Gordon purchased mineral leases on 300,000 acres in Eastland, Stephens, Throckmorton and Palo Pinto Counties. Considering the payments found money and Gordon off his rocker, landowners did not bother to dicker over the price.

The next step was to select two promising sites to drill test wells. Gordon picked Nannie Walker's and John McClesky's farms on the outskirts of Ranger. In August 1917, the Walker well hit gas at 3,200 feet, a real belcher that released ten million cubic feet a day. But it was oil that Gordon was after, and he moved on to the McClesky farm.

By the middle of October, he had run up a tab of $100,000 on the two exploratory wells and only succeeded in testing Edgar Marston's patience. The telegram from New York that Gordon had dreaded did not mince words: "Think we have made a mistake. Better quit." But the true believer had not lost faith and said as much to Texas Pacific's top executive in the same wire in which he asked for more time and more money. Marston relented and granted him full authority to use his own judgment.

Gordon drove directly from the telegraph office in Ranger to the McClesky farm and directed Warren Wagner to resume drilling. Since he was paid by the foot regardless of the result, the instruction was music to the contractor's ears. To save on expenses, Gordon reduced the size of the crew and decided against having steel storage tanks at the ready. In the end, that turned out to be a shortsighted and costly move.

On the afternoon of October 22, 1917, the ground started to shake followed by a barely audible rumbling deep down in the bowels of the earth. The skeleton crew jumped from the platform just as dirt and rock shot out of the hole. Everyone knew what was coming next, so they were not surprised by the fountain of black liquid that rose halfway up the eighty-foot derrick before drenching them from head to toe. Without the storage tanks, no longer a frivolous expense, there was no place for the oil to go other than on the ground. Lacking the equipment to bring the gusher under control, they nailed two boards across the opening and hoped for the best.

The driller and tool dresser strolled into town to call Wagner with the news. People on the street paid them no mind in spite of their oil-soaked appearance. Five minutes later, when the pair walked out of the telephone office, they got everybody's complete attention with the proclamation, "It's an oil well, boys!"

At that very moment, John McCleskey happened to be in town on a shopping trip. Hearing shouts of "There's oil in the McCleskey," he dropped his purchases on the store counter and ran as fast as his sixty-three-year-old legs could carry him to his car. He floorboarded the worn-out Model T all the way home and barreled right through the wood gate at the entrance to his farm. Disbelief turned to pure joy, as McCleskey watched the thing of beauty that would transform his life.

Left: A well in Ranger, one of hundreds. *DeGolyer Library, Southern Methodist University, Texas Postcards Collection.*

Below: In this photograph of Ranger, the town is framed by derricks with smoke rising off in the distance. *Library of Congress.*

Less than twenty-four hours later, in one of those stranger-than-fiction coincidences, the Walker well let out a roar of its own and sent a column of oil over the top of the derrick. No one was present to witness the miraculous occurrence because everybody in Eastland County was over at the McCleskey place celebrating the well-liked farmer's good fortune.

Even though his one-eighth royalty brought in $200 a day for Mr. and Mrs. McCleskey, John was not content to sit back and count his money. Early in the boom, he realized rooms to rent would be a wise investment and built a four-story hotel to meet the demand. The McClesky was where the movers and shakers stayed and made seven- and eight-figure deals in the comfy confines of the spacious lobby.

John McClesky came down with a life-threatening case of typhoid in the summer of 1918. Under the care of the best doctors money could buy, he took a turn for the better only to suffer a relapse and die that July. While he would always be remembered for Ranger's original gusher and the hotel that bore his name, the simple farmer would have given almost anything to have enjoyed his newfound fame and fortune a little longer than nine months.

Merriman, a fly-speck four miles south of Ranger, had been hanging on for dear life since losing the county seat in 1875. In the oil boom, the pitifully few residents saw a chance for a comeback, but Texas Pacific, which had a monopoly on the leases in that neck of the woods, was waiting for the price of oil to rise before drilling. Then along came Warren Wagner, the contractor on the McCleskey well, who had gone into business for himself. An expert at interpreting lease maps, he discovered Texas Pacific had overlooked the acre where the Merriman schoolhouse stood. Money changed hands, and he got busy.

Wagner no sooner positioned his rig and started to sink his hole than the big boys flexed their corporate muscle. Surrounding the schoolhouse site with ten wells, TP's strategy was to suck Wagner's acre dry if he somehow beat them to the punch. For a solid month, everyone worked around the clock, Wagner with his fiercely loyal crew and Texas Pacific with three full shifts. The race ended on the thirty-seventh day, when the underdogs struck oil at 3,200 feet. Victory was sweet in more ways than one, as the schoolhouse well yielded an impressive five thousand barrels a day. By the time TP brought in its first well two weeks later, Wagner was already ahead by $100,000.

Royalty checks were deposited in the Merriman School treasury, which by December 1918 was bursting at the seams with $200,000. Newspapers called the tiny Texas district the wealthiest per capita on the planet, and a former Texas governor chimed in that Merriman had the means to provide every student a high school education and four years at the college of his or her choice. "It could be Oxford, too," Oscar Colquitt proudly boasted.

But in the end, the boom did not change Merriman's destiny. The official population has been fourteen for the past three decades, and most road maps do not even show where it is.

The Ranger boom got off to a slow start. In June 1918, eight months after the McCleskey gusher, daily production had yet to break the four thousand barrels a day barrier. The millions of able-bodied men drafted for the European war that President Wilson had sworn never to fight created a severe labor shortage on the homefront. On top of that, the iron and steel essential to the manufacture of pipelines and storage tanks were diverted by the government to shipyards and munitions plants. Completing a "triple whammy" for the Ranger oilfield was a prolonged drought that left little water for drilling.

The eastward migration of hundreds of families from drought-stricken West Texas eased the manpower shortage, and rain showers replenished the lakes and reservoirs. The workers and water could not have come at more opportune time because, in September, the Ranger field expanded fifteen miles north with a discovery in Stephens County. This was also right about the time the first pipeline reached Ranger, where $5 million worth of crude was ready and waiting.

Ranger had to weather one last storm before shifting into high gear. The influenza epidemic that ravaged the state and the nation in the fall of 1918 did not skip Eastland County, where 2,500 confirmed cases were reported. Some patients perished, most survived and the belated boom finally got on track.

Ranger mushroomed into a bustling beehive of untold thousands before the Christmas holidays—ten, twenty, maybe thirty thousand, no one was keeping score. Even if there had been a method for taking an accurate tally, the figure would have been off by several hundred in less than a day. The night train from Fort Worth looked like a can of human sardines on rails. Men paid full fare to stand in the aisles and on the steps while young daredevils rode on top of the passenger cars. Others came by automobile, when the mud let them, and still more arrived on horseback and on foot. The end mattered, not the means. It didn't matter how they got to Ranger but that they overcame every obstacle standing between them and Texas's El Dorado.

With the McCleskey hotel in the preliminary phase of construction, sleeping quarters were at a premium. A second hotel that was farther along did not let the little things keep them from doing a brisk business. Shown to an unfinished room, a guest complained, "I want to stay here tonight!" The desk clerk smiled knowingly, "It will be ready by then. We are completing the

Ranger from a different angle at the peak of the oil boom. *Library of Congress.*

hotel a room at a time so we can rent each one as rapidly as possible." He paused to let the revelation sink in before collecting three dollars in advance for a room without a door or window panes.

Strangers in tailored suits paid confounded farmers two dollars for the privilege of sharing the barn overnight with the milk cows. In town, the owner of an eight-room residence charged thirty dollars for a cot and had a full house every night.

The roads were a muddy nightmare for days after the skies had cleared. Colonel Robert Gordon, an Eastland merchant no kin to W.K. Gordon, father of the boom, hired a "service car" to drive him the thirty miles

Above: Derricks and an expensive touring car, a symbol of oil prosperity at Ranger. *DeGolyer Library, Southern Methodist University, Texas Postcards Collection.*

Below: Desdemona oilfield as seen from the southeast. *Library of Congress.*

from Cisco to Breckenridge. He paid the driver's thirty-dollar fee with the understanding they would arrive at their destination by four o'clock that afternoon. The first time the car bogged down, half a dozen Good Samaritans came to the rescue. The next time, Gordon coughed up ten dollars to have the vehicle pulled out of a mud hole. After the car experienced mechanical trouble, the merchant walked to the nearest farmhouse, where the sympathetic occupants took him in for the night. Following a good night's rest and a big breakfast—a bargain for five dollars—Gordon talked the farmer into carrying him the remaining ten miles to Cisco in his horse and carriage. The twelve dollars the merchant paid for the last leg of the unforgettable journey brought the total to fifty-seven dollars, or almost two dollars a mile.

But the mire, the shortages and the through-the-roof cost of living did not deter the horde of humanity. Everyone wanted to be among the chosen few who hit the life-changing jackpot, and the stories of those who did fired the imagination and strengthened the resolve of the also-rans.

Word-of-mouth made old Tom Connellee the conflicted hero of the common man. During his twenty-five years as a train conductor, he scrimped and saved to buy 256 acres near Eastland, where he could spend his golden years in solitude. He let a wildcatter have a go at his retirement retreat, as much for the fun of it as the pittance in lease money. Gusher after gusher instigated a bidding war on his front porch that ended with a million-dollar offer for his royalty.

"Nothing doing," storytellers would claim Connellee drawled. "I wouldn't know how to spend a million. What worries me is how to spend the thousand dollars a day I'm getting now."

Tom Harrell, a schoolteacher elected county tax collector on the eve of the boom, was better equipped to handle his windfall. He and his partners turned down $1.2 million for their lease and later thanked their lucky stars they did. Harrell wound up owning six banks, seven lumber yards, three theaters, two hotels and a pipeline company. Those in the know said Harrell was worth $7 million.

Stephen Bethel Strawn started ranching in Palo Pinto County two years before secession and had a hamlet named for him. Alive and kicking at eighty-three, the cowpuncher lived on his royalty riches for the rest of his days.

There were stories that sounded too good to be true, even a century ago: the soldier home from the war in Europe who picked up a lapsed lease for $27 and let a speculator take it off his hands for $50,000 without seeing a drop of oil on the property and the five "colonels" from Kentucky who christened their undertaking by busting a bottle of bourbon on the derrick as a motion-picture camera recorded the bluegrass ritual for posterity. Oil breathed new life into Olden Switch, a hollow shell of a hamlet midway between Ranger and Eastland. The busiest fellow in town was the president of the brand-new bank, a farmer whose days were spent lugging heavy sacks of cash from the express office to his vault.

Before the boom, Desdemona was better off than Olden Switch with a peanut-based economy and a population that fluctuated between three and four hundred. Known by the less pretentious name of Hogtown, it was nestled in the southeastern corner of Eastland County a mile from the border with Comanche County. Owing to the personal popularity of Eugene Debs, who polled close to one million votes in the presidential election of 1912, Desdemona was a socialist stronghold. To pursue their favorite pastime of baseball, the younger socialists and their friends donated one dollar apiece toward the purchase of an acre and a half for a diamond where they regularly beat the daylights out of a team made up of Democrats.

Life in Desdemona revolved around peanuts, socialism and baseball until one fine day in September 1918. Tired of being left out of the boom up north in Ranger, three locals remembered an abandoned well on Hog Creek. Four counties over at Midlothian, there was an oilman who had done right well for himself in the Oklahoma fields, at least according newspaper accounts. It took some convincing, but T.M. Dees reluctantly agreed to investigate the Hog Creek site.

The original wildcatter had plugged the hole with a fence post, which Dees explained would be a waste of time and money to remove. After due deliberation, he settled on an innovative approach with a "star machine," a tried-and-true method of sinking shallow wells, and putting the post to good use as a "bit." Leaving a lone driller behind to handle the job, he went home to tend to a sure thing, his lumberyard.

Word got around Midlothian that Dees had something in the works in Eastland County. On the strength of his reputation alone, a farmer showed up with $3,000 to invest in the venture. One hundred and eight more backers begged Dees to take their money, which he did only when they looked like they could afford to lose it. The enterprise had to have a name, so he called it the Hog Creek Oil Company.

A wealthy investor from Wichita Falls put a fistful of leases at Dees's disposal and left it completely up to him where to drill. He chose the Joe Duke farm south of Desdemona half a mile inside Comanche County. Hogtown was united in the belief that Dees was drilling in the wrong county, but the oilman was deaf to the criticism and kept plugging away.

The ancient adage of "early to bed, early to rise" was faithfully observed in Desdemona. The inhabitants were sound asleep on the night of September 2, 1918, when the loudest noise any had ever heard knocked them out of bed. The source of the explosion was the Duke rig, where a spark had turned a gusher into a tower of fire. The derrick burned so brightly that a night watchman twenty-five miles away in Ranger thought the blaze was on the edge of town. Within minutes, the fire incinerated the wood derrick, leaving in its place a billowing pillar of flame.

The Duke burned for two full days. On the main street of Desdemona, a newspaper could be read at night by the light of the inferno. As soon as Dees and his crew extinguished the fire and brought the flow of oil under control, he took off for Dallas like a bat out of hell. He made the Magnolia Petroleum Company an offer they could not refuse—$700,000 for a half interest in the leases he and his Wichita Falls sponsor held on three thousand acres. Magnolia wrote him a check on the spot, and the fast-thinking oilman had the cash to sink a score of wells on the Duke farm.

To his credit, T.M. Dees did not keep his Midlothian investors waiting. He deducted $150,000 from the Magnolia lump sum to pay the first dividend of the Hog Creek Oil Company.

The wife of Desdemona's one and only physician must have had a heart of gold. The night after the Duke well became a fiery gusher, she looked out the window of their home-office to see forty strangers huddled together in the rain in the vacant lot across the street. She woke her husband with these memorable words: "Millions or no millions, oil or no oil, folks aren't going to have to sleep out in the cold while there are empty beds in my home." The good doctor knew better than to argue

Above: Close-up of Desdemona oilfield on November 19, 1919. *DeGolyer Library, Southern Methodist University, Texas Postcards Collection.*

Below: Panoramic views of the Desdemona field from two different perspectives. *Library of Congress.*

with his mate when she had her mind made up and invited everybody inside for the night.

In contrast to the boom at Ranger, which was dominated by Texas Pacific and other companies with money to burn, Desdemona was where little guys drilling on a hope and a prayer had the chance to try their luck. This crucial difference contributed to the wild, wide-open atmosphere and the anything-goes drilling practices that resulted in an unconscionable waste of a natural resource.

The tremendous gas pressure in the Desdemona field produced more spectacular gushers than anywhere else. The noise could be deafening and, in several instances, did not diminish for days.

The loudest was the Cosden well, which brought the normal activities of daily life to a standstill. "The roar is so great in Desdemona," wrote a correspondent for an out-of-state newspaper, "that conversations are shouted and gesticulated. Talking over the telephone is almost impossible. Mothers can't coo to their babies, and lovemaking is a problem." His final point left a lot to the reader's imagination.

With each passing month, producing wells grew in number. In March 1919, 8 came in, but July recorded a nearly sevenfold increase to 54. The next month, 72 out of 74 struck oil. By October 1919, 300 wells were in

Desdemona was a busy place during the Eastland County boom. *DeGolyer Library, Southern Methodist University, Texas Postcards Collection.*

production or being drilled, with another 750 on hold waiting for equipment. Many believed Desdemona would leave Ranger in the dust and rule the petroleum roost as "the largest known field in the United States and perhaps in the world."

A native of Desdemona returning to his hometown after a year's absence would have thought his eyes were playing tricks on him. The familiar village, where nothing ever changed, had been replaced by a bustling burg bursting at the seams with sixteen thousand people, very few of whom he recognized. The wages would have put a smile on his face with four thousand workers earning from six to twenty-five dollars a day, but the prices would have been a shock to his system. Who had ever heard of a meal of bacon and eggs, potatoes and coffee that cost eighty cents?

But the highlight of his homecoming undoubtedly would have been the good fortune that had befallen "salt of the earth" folks he had known since childhood. Take, for example, the mother and daughter, both widows, whose land was smack-dab in the middle of the pool. For openers, they received $135,000 in lease payments and stood to make as much as $5 million in royalties. After selling his farm for $250,000, an elderly settler hired out as a helper around the rig on his former place for $5 a day. Asked by astonished acquaintances why he continued to work, the man said, "I can save the principal and live on the five-spot." The

Traffic was bad in Desdemona but knee-deep water in the streets was worse. *MSS0100-0024, Houston Public Library, HMRC.*

Three automobiles stuck in the mud up to the axles on a Desdemona street. *DeGolyer Library, Southern Methodist University, Texas Postcards Collection.*

first thing a second old man planned on buying with his oil money was meat for his thirteen dogs. After that, he would purchase the biggest red automobile he could find and take his beloved canines for a ride. Another Hogtown pioneer, whose bank balance was pushing seven figures, wanted "to build a house on the Stephenville road so I can see what's going on."

Every oil boomtown lived with the constant threat of fire. In Desdemona the volunteer brigade was called upon twice in five days to battle two huge blazes with nothing more than water buckets and wet blankets. The first consumed two hotels, two tailor shops, a café and a general store before the part-time firemen got the better of it. A strong wind gave the second fire a head-start on the volunteers, who fought the flames for three exhausting hours before eventually saving what was left of the town. Ashes were all that remained of the town's two theaters, two more hotels, three diners, a pair of garages, two drugstores, two grocery stores, a barbershop and a dry goods store. A ballpark estimate of the loss came to almost $2 million in twenty-first-century dollars.

As boomtowns went, Desdemona was a rough place but no worse than most and not as bad as others. Oilfield workers, especially the soldiers who had faced death in the trenches of war-torn Europe, did not brook insults or mistreatment of any sort.

"Fire Ranger Texas. Sun Night April 6, 1919." *DeGolyer Library, Southern Methodist University, Texas Postcards Collection.*

"Desdemona's latest sport, sight-seeing from the clouds." *DeGolyer Library, Southern Methodist University, Texas Postcards Collection.*

The city marshal, accustomed to throwing his weight around, should have taken that into account when he decided to show the disrespectful rowdies who was boss. Looking for a way to get a rise out of the veterans, he defaced a poster with a picture of the American Legion commander and walked down Main Street daring the vets to do something about it. A group of sixty ex-soldiers and roughnecks stopped the lawman and his deputy and told them in no uncertain terms to surrender their firearms.

Realizing he had bitten off much more than he could chew, the marshal nevertheless hoped to save face. "Is there an officer in the crowd?" he inquired shaking in his boots. A so-called special Ranger came forward, identified himself and accepted their weapons. At this point, a voice in the throng shouted, "Ride 'em out of town on a rail!" But cooler heads prevailed, and the humiliated marshal and his sidekick were allowed to leave Desdemona unharmed.

Ranger and Desdemona may have been hogging all the attention, but Stephens County was having a heck of an oil boom, too. Drilling crews picked up the scent and followed it north out of Eastland County to crossroad

Above: Stephens County village of Necessity during the brief better days of the oil boom. *Library of Congress.*

communities with colorful names like Gunsight, Necessity, Frankell, Leeray and Caddo.

The eight hundred people in Breckenridge worried and wondered when, or if, their turn would come. They had fallen on hard times of late as the drought dried up the grassland that cattlemen depended on for grazing their herds. Family after family had moved out to search for greener pastures—literally, not figuratively—leaving their homes standing vacant since there were no buyers. The decrease in population resulted in fewer and fewer customers for the merchants, and the blight of boarded-up storefronts infected the downtown business district.

Opposite: "Breckenridge, Texas burning again. The dread of an oil town—fire!" *DeGolyer Library, Southern Methodist University, Texas Postcards Collection.*

Below, top: The town a stone's throw from the Red River and the oilfield were named for rancher Burk Burnett by his personal friend Teddy Roosevelt. *Library of Congress.*

Below, bottom: "The World's Wonder Oil Field" may have overstated the size and importance of the Burkburnett boom, but it lasted longer than most. *Library of Congress.*

Right: The town of Burkburnett is nowhere in sight in this January 1919 photograph of the oilfield. *Library of Congress.*

Above: Burkburnett "showing 8 months phenomenal development." The movie *Boom Town*, starring Clark Gable, was loosely based on events that followed 1912 discovery. *Library of Congress.*

Opposite: Trucks and horse-drawn wagons haul equipment into the west field at Burkburnett. *MSS0243-1020, Houston Public Library, HMRC.*

February 4, 1918, was a red-letter day in the history of Breckenridge. The struggling settlement breathed a lot easier after the crew on "No. 1 Chaney" brought in a big-time gusher. The familiar boomtown bounce was repeated as the population jumped to thirty thousand. Two hundred wells were drilled inside the town limits, and the barrel count surpassed ten million by the end of year. Breckenridge proved to be no flash-in-the-pan, as production tripled over the next two years. Long after the Eastland County boom had bottomed out, two thousand rigs kept the town that had come close to going under hitting on all cylinders.

BURNETT TEXAS
202 1919

ON THE HIGHWAY IN THE FAMOUS NORTH-WEST FIELD BURKBURNETT TEXAS

Top: The Burk Waggoner Pool was a joint venture by ranching rivals Burk Burnett and W.T. Waggoner. *Library of Congress*.

Bottom: The caption of this photograph, taken at Burkburnett, states simply "Big Production." *Library of Congress*.

In the year and a half since the McClesky gusher, only one murder had been committed in Ranger, which had to be a record for a Texas town in the eye of an oil hurricane. Just when residents began to think they were immune to the violence that seemed part and parcel of the boomtown lifestyle, rivers of blood started to flow and inspired the repugnant nickname of "Roarin' Ranger."

Killings became so common that every street in town soon had its story of sudden death from the barrel of a gun. Four lives were extinguished within a block of city hall and six on a single residential street. As the wave of violence broke over the town, five men were shot dead on one weekend.

"Lackadaisical" was the word that best described law enforcement in Ranger. In one of the rare instances when the perpetrator was arrested, jailed and charged, the accused had cut a man "from ear to ear" in a knife attack. After a cursory review of the evidence, the judge concluded the chances of conviction were slim to none if the case went to trial. So with a wave of his judicial wand, he changed the charge to vagrancy and instructed the bailiff to bring in the defendant:

Looking down the back street in Kilgore known as "Six-Shooter Alley." *DeGolyer Library, Southern Methodist University, Texas Postcards Collection.*

You can't come into our peaceful little community and strike down one of our leading citizens and not expect to feel the weighty hand of the law. I fine you 75 dollars and I want this to be a lesson to you. Get out of town and let your first stop be Shanghai, China. If you ever assassinate another of our citizens, I'll give you the full limit of the court—250 dollars and costs. Call the next case.

After that and other courtroom comedies, Ranger got a reputation as a wide-open town, where enforcement of the law was lax and punishment was a joke. Crime was such a growing industry that the law-abiding, who even on the most violent days constituted a majority, were afraid to walk the streets. Pressure was brought to bear on public officials to find somebody with the backbone to beat the criminals at their own game.

That man was Byron Parrish. A native of Mason in the Hill Country, he had been employed by a governor as his personal bodyguard, bested the dregs of humanity in border towns on the Rio Grande and most recently had served with distinction in the Texas Rangers. He accepted the offer from the besieged city fathers in Ranger not for the money but for their promise of a free hand in ridding the boomtown of the dangerous criminal element.

Parrish was a master of the art of first impressions. In his 1935 book *Were You in Ranger?*, Boyce House presented this spellbinding picture of Parrish's gaudy get-up on that day in 1919 when he rode into the boomtown:

> *His suits were tailor-made, usually of blue serge, though sometimes he wore gray or brown. A white shirt, a four-in-hand tie, made-to-order boots, high-heeled, with fancy-stitched designs, and a big white hat with a clover leaf emblem on each side. Gold pieces were used as cuff links and shirt studs. A larger gold piece formed a stickpin and largest of all was the gold coin that dangled from his heavy watch chain. A big diamond glittered on his right hand and a heavy amethyst was on the other hand.*
>
> *A heavy belt filled with cartridges bore at each hip a specially made holster, well-worn with use, and each held a Smith & Wesson six-shooter, pearl-handled, inlaid with gold, the barrels of gleaming nickel.*

Although the position of chief of police was his for the asking, Parrish preferred the entry-level post of deputy constable. Ranger had gone through four chiefs in six months, and he did not want to be the fifth because he

Ranger when it was riding the crest of the boom no one thought would ever end. *Library of Congress.*

neglected to take the time to study the cast of characters and their favorite haunts. As soon as he knew the boomtown inside and out, he pinned on the badge he had been hired to wear.

The first step was to ban the carrying of firearms inside the city limits. Everyone, the good and the bad, walked the streets armed. Parrish did not humiliate anybody by taking away his gun in public but made it clear that, in the future, the offender would be well advised to leave his weapon at home. The new chief's firearms policy convinced numerous bad actors that it was time to move along.

Without revolvers at their fingertips, disputes were settled with fists instead of bullets. The murder rate dropped to near zero, and Ranger no longer roared. Nonetheless, Chief Parrish had no illusions that he could bring a lasting peace to the boomtown without putting the local crime lord in his place. That, too, was accomplished without a shot being fired, though he did have to resort to an old border-town tactic: a hard blow to the head with the barrel of his six-shooter. The skull-splitting took the fight out of the outlaw, who vanished, never to be seen again on the streets of Ranger.

With the remaining petty crooks, cardsharps and prostitutes on their best behavior, Parrish did not know what to do with himself. He took to drinking, his customary cure for boredom, which resulted in irrational fits of temper and violent outbursts. The flogging with a wet rope of a respected businessman for allegedly "running around on his wife" was the last straw for the townspeople who three months before had hailed him as their savior. By unanimous vote, the city council fired him as chief of police.

The Associated Press reported in June 1931 that Byron Parrish, fifty-five, dropped dead on the street in Rankin, a small West Texas town south of Midland. The official cause of death was "excessive use of alcohol."

TEXAS BOOMTOWNS

No inquest was needed to determine what caused the boom in Eastland County to go bust. At Ranger, it was like the disgraced chief of police had pulled the plug on his way out of town. The oil ran out, the pumps went dry and the good times stopped rolling in the fall of 1920. The economy went into a tailspin, taking the banks and most businesses with it. From a probable high of 30,000, the population nose-dived to 6,200 by the end of the decade, and eighty years later, census takers could find no more than 2,500 inhabitants. As for Desdemona, the bottom dropped out at the same time for the same reasons and with the same outcome. Today, Hogtown is home to 180 die-hards.

3

BOOM BROUGHT A
WORLD OF TROUBLE

The larger-than-life stranger sure knew how to make an entrance. Colonel Albert E. Humphreys, all 240 impeccably dressed pounds of him, bounded off the train at Mexia, Texas, and landed with a rafter-rattling thud on the wood-plank platform. With every head in the station turned in his direction, the "King of the Wildcatters" announced himself in his booming baritone.

"Hello, everybody! I'm Colonel Humphreys of Virginia, and I am here to help you find oil!"

For many of the startled spectators, no introduction was necessary, even though the center of attention had never set foot in the Central Texas town. They instantly recognized one of the most famous and most photographed men in America. For the benefit of those who drew a blank on his face and name that autumn day in 1919, friends explained that the Colonel had made and lost fabulous fortunes in Virginia timber; Minnesota iron ore; Canadian gold; and, more recently, oil in Oklahoma, Wyoming and Louisiana. And if Albert Humphreys had gone to the trouble of coming to their off-the-beaten-track community, it could only mean the rumors of oil in Limestone County had to be true.

That's not to say Mexia (pronounced muh-hay-uh) was in any danger of drying up and blowing away after the Great War. A stable community of 3,500 inhabitants one hundred miles south of Fort Worth, it was where cotton farmers from miles around brought their crop to be ginned and sold. Most Mexiaites, white and black, managed to get by and some even prospered, so it was not like the small town needed oil to survive. But it sure would be nice, or so it seemed at the start.

The boom began not in Mexia or even Limestone County, but ten miles to the north in the county next door called Freestone. A water well was drilled sometime in 1913 at the hamlet of Wortham but hit gas and oil instead. However, those finds soon played out, and the accidental discovery was chalked off as a freak of nature.

Or it was by everyone but Blake Smith, a twenty-something cashier in a Mexia bank who could think of nothing else. His day job brought him into contact with every man of means in town, and he was not the least bit shy about broaching the subject of drilling for oil with every single one of them. Some laughed in his face, and others advised him to forget about it. But Smith persisted and, in time, persuaded a handful of businessmen to put up the money for ten exploratory wells.

Calling themselves the Mexia Oil and Gas Company, the bank cashier and his gray-haired partners hired an experienced contractor willing to work cheap. He drilled nine holes and each turned out dry. With his dream hanging by a thread, Blake Smith made him "a sporting proposition." "You owe us one more well," he said to the contractor. "Drill two for the same money, but you need not drill as deep."

The old roughneck may have felt sorry for the bright-eyed kid, or maybe he had nothing better to do. Whatever the reason, he agreed to sink two more wells at the specified depth. When both were as bone-dry as the previous nine, he insisted Smith drive out to the lease with him to see for himself. Only then, the contractor reasoned, would the eternal optimist accept the fact he had been wrong.

Blake Smith stepped out of the car with a lump in his throat. He stared at the eleventh and last hole and watched it bubble. It took him, as well as the confused contractor, a minute or two to understand what was happening. When it finally sank in, Smith exclaimed, "Look at that! It's gas!"

The gas deposit satisfied the needs of Mexia and other towns in the area for a number of years and rewarded the teller's partners with a handsome return on their investment. Blake Smith was pleased with his share of the profits but disappointed by his failure to find what he was really looking for—oil. With the blessing of his fat and happy partners, the young man arranged for a new contractor to resume drilling on the lease, but he ran out of money before reaching the desired depth.

That was when Albert Humphreys entered the picture. Smith and the trusting residents of Mexia wanted to believe he was rolling in money, so the cagey Colonel let them. The truth was that the high-roller had run through the bulk of his latest fortune and needed a big score more than they did. Dazzling suppliers with his reputation, he obtained all the equipment essential to drilling a well and retreated to an island off the Texas Gulf coast before anyone had a chance to ask him to pay up.

Colonel Humphreys passed the time fishing and scanning the shoreline for the afternoon flag-raising by a confederate. A white banner meant nothing to report, while a red flag signaled pay dirt had been struck. After frustrating weeks of white flags, Humphreys at last spotted a red pennant flapping in the Gulf breeze in early November 1920.

The Colonel rushed back to Mexia in triumph, and with the proceeds from the ice-breaker to pay concerned creditors, began building a 1,600-barrel storage tank and leased seventeen thousand acres for the next phase of his double-or-nothing gamble. Although Humphreys made a big deal out of his success, word got out that it was strictly small potatoes with a puny flow of 50 barrels a day. That did not amount to a boom in anybody's book and caused skeptics to wonder out loud whether the wildcatter had lost his magic touch.

Six months later, in May 1921, Humphreys-Henry No. 1 came in less than a mile from the first well. With a daily flow of three thousand barrels, it renewed the fading hope of Mexiaites that the Colonel might be on to something after all.

By the end of July, more than seventy derricks, the majority sporting Humphreys's trademark H on a Confederate-gray background, dotted the landscape. Everyone, prospectors and townspeople alike, nervously waited for the dramatic event that would demonstrate beyond any doubt that Mexia was indeed the site of Texas's next big oil boom.

Proof positive came in the form of twin gushers that roared to life on August 29, 1921. Two miles northwest of town, the Julius Desenberg No. 1 already was spewing a black fountain at a daily rate of eighteen thousand barrels when the W.L. Adamson No. 1 erupted with the earth-shaking force of a volcano that blew away the derrick like a Tinker Toy. Engineers at the crude-covered scene calculated the flow again and again before they had sufficient confidence in the number to announce it to the crowd: one thousand barrels an *hour*.

Julius Desenberg No. 1, one of the twin gushers that signaled the start of the Mexia boom on August 29, 1921. *DeGolyer Library, Southern Methodist University, Texas Postcards Collection.*

BOOM BROUGHT A WORLD OF TROUBLE

The news from Central Texas could not have come at a better time, for thousands of oilfield workers and camp followers idled by the busted booms at Ranger, Desdemona and Burkburnett. The race was on, and Mexia was hit a few days later by a human tidal wave that increased its population ten times over.

With 35,000 people instead of the normal 3,500 clamoring for the necessities of life, there was a severe shortage of everything.

Everyone had to sleep, but the problem was where. Those lucky enough to rent a hotel room for the night paid eight dollars for a "double." That was not a room with two beds but one bed for two guests, who more likely than not had never laid eyes on each other. The only rule, strictly enforced by innkeepers, was muddy boots had to be removed before crawling into bed. When the night shift vacated the premises bright and early the next morning, day sleepers took their place at the same eight-dollar rate but without the benefit of fresh bed linen.

The handful of hotels, four at most, rented chairs in their lobbies when they ran out of rooms, which happened every evening. One hotel, the Commercial, provided late-comers with overnight accommodations in "Room 15," a tongue-in-cheek term for a two-and-a-half-dollar cot in the hall.

Many of those turned away by the hotels went door to door pleading with homeowners to take them in for the night. Some hit the jackpot with long-term bed-and-breakfast plans that ranged in price from fifty to one hundred dollars weekly. Everyone else was left with no other choice but to catch forty winks in the great outdoors. Several thousand spent the night at "Mrs. Sprawl's," slang for the railroad park, where grass was the mattress and newspaper the blanket. The lawns of private homes also served as "crash pads" for squatters, who neither asked permission nor paid for the privilege of dozing on private property.

It did not take long for the migrant workers to tire of bedding down under the stars or paying through the nose for a room. The alternative was a "shotgun shack" that could be thrown together in two or three hours with nothing more than two-by-fours, tar paper and tin for the roof. The wide-open space between the western city limits and the edge of the oilfield rapidly filled up with cheap hovels hardly fit for human habitation.

In the meantime, more substantial structures were being constructed at an unprecedented pace. At the end of the fourth month of the boom, when the population peaked around fifty thousand, the mayor revealed that 3,350 building permits had been issued. To put that figure into perspective, he noted it was more than all the permits issued in the half century since the founding of Mexia.

No shortage was more dire than that of water, which posed a serious threat to public health. A water system designed for a community less than one-twelfth the current size could not keep up with demand. As a result, the town went without water all day until the tap was turned on at eight o'clock in the evening for cooking, washing and bathing. It stayed open all night, but there usually was not a drop left in the pipes when the tap was officially shut off at six o'clock the next morning.

Scarcity invariably puts money in somebody's pocket, and in this case, it was enterprising boys. Lads toting around two pails of water were a common sight on Mexia streets, where they earned ten to twenty dollars a day selling the precious refreshment by the glass.

The post office was a madhouse. Before the double gushers turned his world upside down, Postmaster Billie W. Simmons had no trouble handling the incoming and outgoing mail with a staff of four, counting himself. But as soon as the boom began, he could not keep up regardless of how much help he hired.

Simmons spent a big chunk of his day begging and borrowing stamps from other post offices in North and Central Texas. He put several new hires to work at night sorting the mountain of mail, but they never seemed to put a dent in it. He tried opening earlier and closing later to assist the patrons standing in a long line for "general delivery," but it never got any shorter.

Suffering from a bad case of burnout, Simmons tried to resign but Washington would not send a replacement. He eventually got the attention of the postmaster general with this telegram: "If you don't have someone on hand to check me out next Monday, I'll lock up the post office and throw away the keys."

As always happened during the start-up stage of a major oil boom, drilling companies struggled with a constant shortage of pipe and other indispensable equipment. At Mexia, the problem stemmed not from a lack of supplies but a transportation bottleneck on the highways and rail lines into the oilfield.

Heavily loaded horse-drawn wagons and trucks moved at a snail's pace down narrow two-lane dirt roads. When the rains came and turned the black soil into an impassable morass, the caravans were bogged down completely. On those occasions, desperate drillers would dispatch armed men to fetch their shipments by any means necessary. Sometimes they resorted to outright theft of equipment destined for a rival, resulting in blazing gun battles.

The two railroads that connected Mexia with Houston and Dallas lacked the tracks to move the freight on anything remotely resembling a schedule. Thirty-six clerks and fourteen switch engines working around the clock for Southern Pacific could not come close to handling the sheer volume of shipments. A retired telegrapher recalled thirty-five years later that in one particular month, total receipts for Mexia were second only to San Francisco in the entire SP system.

Drinking water, a roof over their heads and a bed for the night may have been hard to come by for the "boomers," but there was more than enough booze, gambling, women and bloodshed to go around.

The Eighteenth Amendment to the U.S. Constitution took effect on January 16, 1920, twenty months before the twin gushers started the mad dash for Mexia. Prohibition made it a crime in every state, county and community in the country to manufacture, sell and consume alcoholic beverages. But in the wide-open boomtown, and those like it that cropped up before repeal in December 1933, it was like the Volstead Act had never been put on the books.

As derricks sprouted like weeds in the open fields west of Mexia, so did shacks, similar in appearance to the "shotgun" variety, that offered bootleg whiskey, poker, craps and other rigged games that never gave a sucker an even break, along with the oldest diversion of all, prostitution. The red-light district reminded oilfield laborers so much of the Mexican border town opposite El Paso that they named it "Juarez." From their segregated neighborhood on the west side of town, blacks watched with rising anxiety as Juarez grew by leaps and bounds in their direction. Rather than wait for the cancer to spread to their streets, black Mexiaites packed up and moved clear across town.

Juarez was where working stiffs with oil on their faces and mud on their boots went to blow off steam after long back-breaking shifts. Fistfights were a form of entertainment and usually fought to the finish since nobody bothered to separate the combatants. Murder, sometimes for hire, was also a nightly occurrence that resulted in a new routine for the police, the crack-of-dawn collection of the dead from back alleys.

The Winter Garden and the Chicken Farm catered to a more upscale clientele with wallets fat from instant riches. The Winter Garden was a casino, restaurant and dance hall—the old frontier euphemism for brothel—four miles east of Mexia on the Teague highway. Built in an open space 250 yards from the busy road, it featured the best liquor money could buy, the prettiest "dancers" and games unavailable in Juarez like roulette and black jack. No expense was spared in providing security for the protection of the customers and, more importantly, the operators, whose nightly take was in the tens of thousands of dollars. Cars turning onto the country lane leading to the Winter Garden were stopped by armed guards and searched inside and out for weapons. Customers submitted to a second TSA-like frisk at the door before being granted entrance to the premises. Once inside, more guards with even bigger guns watched for any sign of trouble from card cheats to oil tycoons who could not handle their liquor.

But when it came to security, the Chicken Farm made the competition look like pikers. Strategically positioned just over the Limestone County line in Freestone County, the fortress stood on land bought from a deputy sheriff, who later swore on a stack of Bibles that he had no idea what the new owner planned on doing with it. In the center of the club was a concrete cylinder with the barrels of hunting rifles protruding from custom-built gun ports. Nothing in the enormous room escaped the attention of the guards at the other end of the barrels. Behind the bar and out of sight were two trapdoors designed for emergency use in the event of a raid. The smaller was for quick disposal of the ocean of illegal hooch, and the larger was an escape route for club personnel and patrons deemed too delicate to spend a night in jail.

The "good stuff" served to the refined palates at the Winter Garden and the Chicken Farm came from Canada and Europe by way of Galveston. Speedboats deposited cases on the beach by the light of the moon, and smugglers delivered the shipments by truck to the two most notorious nightspots in the whole state of Texas.

The blue-collar crowd in Juarez was only interested in getting drunk as cheaply and as fast as possible and was willing to risk blindness and "jake leg," paralysis of the lower limbs, to do it. Their favorite poison was "White Mule," a specialty of the moonshiners in Freestone County and southern Limestone County who cooked up the concoction with their backwoods stills. White Mule cost two and a half dollars a pint on the streets of Juarez and not even the hardest drinkers went back for seconds.

BOOM BROUGHT A WORLD OF TROUBLE

In her thirteen-part series on the boom times in Mexia that ran in the *Waco Times-Herald* in 1955, Nanine Simmons described in fascinating detail the wily ways of two clever bootleggers. The first

> *traded only with a select, restricted list of customers, who would drive out to his farm and take a pre-arranged look around his deserted yard. They took delivery by turning up a washtub or taking off the top of a teakettle, and there was their bottle waiting for them.*
>
> *Once a week, he'd come out of the woods where his still was to hear the oil news and make his rounds to collect. Because his regulars all knew his corn had never poisoned any yet, there was never any trouble about his collecting in full.*

The second bootlegger took a more direct approach by conducting his business in the very heart of Mexia. "A pair of overalls that hung in the doorway of a busy downtown garage was another popular counter for those bathtub wares," Simmons wrote. "You could reach in its pocket, help yourself, substitute its price and be gone in the throng of the street in about as long as it took to nod to a mechanic. And with about as much danger."

Though in his early sixties, Colonel Albert Humphreys was a tireless bundle of energy who never seemed to sleep. He was bound and determined to recoup his earlier losses in one fell swoop and take his leave of Mexia with the biggest fortune of his flamboyant career. But in sharp contrast to the typical tycoon, who thought of nobody but himself, Humphreys left the Texas town in much better shape than he found it.

Less than six months after the historic strikes of August 1921, the Colonel had his own private empire with 150 rigs and eighty-eight steel storage tanks with a combined capacity of five million barrels. His wells pumped $100,000 worth of black gold every twenty-four hours, a river of crude that amounted to a monthly income of three million dollars.

Humphreys shared the wealth with his two thousand employees. He paid them top wages and bestowed benefits that included company housing, three square meals a day and medical care in a hospital, one of Texas's best, which he built and operated at his own expense.

As a loyal son of the Old South, Colonel Humphreys endeared himself to the people of Mexia with his devotion to the "Lost Cause." In the initial phase of his renovation of the Confederate Reunion Grounds, established by returning Rebs as a place for their nostalgic get-togethers, he built a pavilion and public bathhouse. He followed that generous gesture with the construction of a clubhouse rumored to have cost as much as $100,000, which he gave to the stunned-speechless community at the grand opening.

All that Humphreys asked in return was the right to divert water from Jack's Creek and the Navasota River to his thirsty oil operation. In light of his big-hearted gifts, grateful Mexiaites could hardly say no. From that day on, the Colonel had free and unlimited access to all the water he could use, which gave him a critical leg up on the competition.

Besides town benefactor, Humphreys was Mexia's Pied Piper in a brown suit, a role he relished. Whenever a well was about to blow, he put on the same duds he wore to welcome his first gusher and hurried into town to give everybody the news. Before the Colonel even opened his mouth, they could tell from the color of his clothes what was going on. Hundreds if it was a weekday or thousands on the weekend would drop what they were doing and follow him out to the field to watch the well blow its top. Like their Barnum of a ringmaster, the people of Mexia never tired of the exciting sight.

In his role as entertainer-in-chief, Colonel Humphreys invited everybody who was anybody to come see him in Mexia. The most famous visitor was General John J. "Black Jack" Pershing, commander of the American Expeditionary Force in the European bloodbath referred to as the Great War. Texans remembered Pershing from the year he spent in Mexico hunting Pancho Villa only to return red-faced and empty-handed, a humiliating failure that did not stop President Woodrow Wilson from putting the lives of the "doughboys" in his hands.

General Pershing arrived in January 1922 with seventy-five traveling companions, who included Charles Dawes, the next vice-president of the United States. Humphreys could not wait to show off his latest project, the first paved road in Limestone County that ran from the Groesbeck Highway past the antebellum mansion the Colonel had spent $35,000 restoring to the Confederate Reunion Grounds. In the presence of the grinning general, the ribbon of asphalt was christened the "Pershing Way."

That evening under the bright lights of the clubhouse, Pershing and his entourage, plus two dozen lucky Mexiaites, feasted on duck, yams, bacon and beans, cranberry sauce, dressing, cornbread, coffee and pie. Naturally, Albert Humphreys picked up the tab, conservatively estimated at $7,000.

Learning from his past mistake of staying in the game too long, the Colonel cashed in his chips in early 1923. He got $7 million for a fourth of his Mexia holdings and $30 million for the balance. He hung around long enough to open new fields at Wortham in Freestone County and Nocona, a stone's throw from the Red River, and to drill the oddball gusher at Kosse that spewed forty-eight thousand barrels in forty-eight hours before stopping all of a sudden like some invisible hand had turned it off. And with that, Colonel Albert E. Humphreys bid Texas farewell.

Humphreys was the undisputed "king" of the Mexia wildcatters, but there were others deserving of the title "prince." Chief among them was J.K. Hughes, a native Texan who was treading water with a hardware store and lumberyard near Temple when he heard about the excitement at Mexia. He headed for the boomtown with less than five bucks in his pocket and the two diamonds from his wife's wedding ring.

By the time Hughes joined the mob scene in Mexia, all the premium leases were taken. The available tracts were cheaper than dirt merely because no one who knew the first thing about chasing crude thought there was oil west of the original discovery. Hughes could turn around and go home or gamble his glittery grubstake on the unwanted leases. He converted the diamonds into cash, bought every lease he could and began drilling with what little money he had left.

When two wells within sight of Hughes's turned into gushers, an eager operator offered him $100,000 for the drilling rights to the fifty acres on the Ellis farm that had cost him $7,500, but Hughes turned the man down. At this point, his three silent partners spoke up to ask if he had lost his ever-loving mind. Hughes assured them he had all his marbles at last count and, as an afterthought, informed them the operator had upped his bid to $250,000. When the color at last returned to their faces, the trio said in unison, "A lease that can be sold for a quarter of a million dollars is worth keeping."

Hughes held his ground as a bidding frenzy raised the offer to the dizzy height of $1.5 million. After his stubborn stand was rewarded with a strike, he drilled thirteen simultaneous wells and hit oil with an even dozen. His lucky streak stayed intact at Mildred and Powell, crossroad communities southeast of Corsicana, and in short order he had one hundred wells in production.

After his unscrupulous partners wrested control of the original company from him, Hughes bounced back by building a second that he sold for $5 million. In refreshing contrast to the get-rich-quick breed that took the money and ran, Hughes and his wife made Mexia their home for life. When the boom hit the unavoidable brick wall, he did his part to take up the economic slack by opening a textile mill that generated jobs and helped the town kick the oil habit. The civic-minded oilman donated twelve acres for a city park and played a major part in the creation of a county club. Hughes took particular pride in the fact that one of his companies paid an annual dividend of 400 percent from 1922 through 1927 and another declared dividends of 100 percent per month for five years.

The stars of an assortment of rags-to-riches sagas were simple folk, who stumbled onto the pot at the end of the rainbow. An unusual number of black Mexiaites benefitted from the boom because they had clear title to the land they plowed. Since the black community as a whole owned the eighteen acres where the annual Juneteenth celebration was held, everyone received an equal share of the $45,000 drilling lease. A druggist, who paid $2,000 for the fifty-five acres he farmed in his spare time, skipped town clutching a check for $1.25 million. A teacher made more in royalties every day of the week than she earned in a year in the classroom. A few years earlier, a group of fifteen men paid $65 apiece to fish and paddle their boats in the town reservoir. When a gusher was drilled on the bank of the shallow waterhole, they split $700,000. The most heartwarming story involved a school principal with a severely handicapped son. Although he declined to divulge the dimensions of his windfall, he freely admitted to putting every cent of the first $100,000 payment into government bonds for the boy's future and the special equipment that enabled him to drive an automobile.

There were, of course, many examples of the "nouveau riche" who went through their wealth like green grass through a Texas steer. A white farmer, who rarely had two nickels to rub together, bought a string of red Pierce Arrows trading in the current model the moment it got dirty. For those who neglected to put money aside for a rainy day, the newfangled income tax came as quite a shock. When his banker told a free-spending farmer for the umpteenth time that the government was not kidding about his delinquent tax bill, he finally got the man's attention by letting him know he was entitled to a one-thousand-dollar deduction for his wife. "What about all those other women?" exclaimed the farmer. "They're costing me lots more than my old woman!"

For the 99 percent who did not hit the oilfield lottery, there was ample opportunity to earn more money than they had ever seen before or would ever see again in their hardworking lives. A Central Texas family in the early '20s could live rather well on eighty-five dollars a month. However, when the breadwinner caught on with Humphreys, Hughes or another drilling

BOOM BROUGHT A WORLD OF TROUBLE

"Waiting for the tide to go down Mexia, Texas." *DeGolyer Library, Southern Methodist University, Texas Postcards Collection.*

company, their lives changed for the better overnight. Rig builders and drillers pulled down twenty-five dollars a day and took a day off maybe once in a blue moon. The going daily rate for tool dressers was twenty bucks, and unskilled day laborers could count on twelve to fifteen dollars at quitting time. But far too many oilfield workers did not make it home with their hard-earned wages because they could not resist the temptations of the Juarez sin pit.

Merchants, small businesses and every occupation under the hot Texas sun benefitted from the ripple effect of the infusion of oil dollars into the Mexia economy. Horse and mule drawn wagons could go places trucks could not. Drivers with their own teams and wagons demanded one hundred dollars a day and were worth every penny. When rain storms turned the dirt roads into impassable quagmires, farmers cut holes in their barbed wire fences and charged a dollar per vehicle for the privilege of taking the shortcut through their pastures.

Waitresses, who in normal times struggled to keep body and soul together, took home as much as fifty dollars a shift in tips. The women were a familiar sight in their knee-high boots and mink coats, the former needed for wading through the muddy streets and the latter extravagant tokens of appreciation from wealthy oilmen.

A small segment of the indigenous inhabitants of Mexia never jumped on the oil-boom bandwagon. The reason varied from person to person. Some already had a comfortable and secure existence and feared change of any kind would upset the applecart. Others were pious churchgoers and hard-core Prohibitionists who had heard about the moral toll the oil insanity had taken on Ranger, Desdemona, Burkburnett and other Northwest Texas communities. Whatever their differences, the "anti's" were united by the conviction that the boom was certain to bring a world of trouble to Mexia.

In the new governor, who had been in office only seven months when the twin gushers blew in, the naysayers hoped to find a sympathetic ear. To that end, they began a letter-writing campaign that steadily grew in strength as their numbers increased. But they need not to have worried about Pat Neff since he was one of them to his core.

Elected to the Texas legislature from Waco at the age of twenty-seven, the Baylor graduate looked to be on the fast track to high office. After being sworn in for his third term in 1903, Neff became the youngest Speaker of the House by vote of his Democratic peers. Two years later, he mystified his colleagues and the voters back home by refusing to run for reelection, choosing a private law practice in Waco over a promising career in state and possibly even national politics.

Neff's admirers virtually drafted him for McLennan County attorney, but in office, he warmed up to the idea. Of the 422 cases he tried over the next six years, he won convictions in all but 16. True to his Prohibitionist principles, he was the first prosecutor in Texas to send a bootlegger to prison.

After more than a decade of his self-imposed political exile, Neff up and decided in 1919 to run for governor. If the incumbent had loved politics instead of the newspaper business, Neff would not have had a snowball's chance. But William P. Hobby bowed out, and Joseph Weldon Bailey, the former U.S. senator who seven years earlier had resigned in disgrace, took his place as the odds-on favorite.

Neff started his uphill campaign with little support, even less money and no organization. He crisscrossed the vast state alone in his own personal car giving as many as seven speeches a day in 152 of the 254 counties. In 37 counties, people presumed he had taken a wrong turn because no gubernatorial candidate in history had shown his face there.

Neff broke with the long-standing Texas tradition of not mixing politics and religion by campaigning as a proud and unapologetic "hard-shell"

Baptist. (As President Garfield lay dying from an assassin's bullet and his doctors' incompetence in 1881, Governor Oran Roberts refused to order a day of prayer because it would violate the separation of church and state.) But it was Neff's strait-laced morality and personal eccentricities that attracted the most ridicule and charges that he "was not man enough" to govern Texas. Typical of the attacks was this editorial in the *Quanah Observer*: "Neff has never shot a gun. He has never baited a fishhook. He has never touched tobacco in any form. He does not know one card from another and he cannot play any kind of social game. Pattie wore lace on his nighties and was never known to be away from home after sundown."

In his unsullied prime, Joe Bailey would have trounced Pat Neff without breaking a sweat. The few true believers who stood by the old warhorse cast enough ballots to give him a narrow lead in the opening round of the 1920 Democratic Party primary but could not stop the crusading challenger from sweeping their fallen hero aside in the runoff.

The way Pat Neff saw it, the voters of Texas knew what they were getting when they elected him governor—a man of faith with a strict moral code and zero tolerance for drinking, gambling and whoring in open defiance of the statutes of the state and the nation. It was not a question of if he would clean up Mexia but when.

Governor Neff was ready to move against the boomtown lawbreakers by December 1921 but did not want to go off half-cocked. Any decision to intervene had to be based on facts rather than the emotional appeals and anecdotal evidence from the letter-writers. To that end, he ordered Adjutant General Thomas D. Barton of the Texas National Guard to send his best agent to Mexia on an undercover investigation.

Governor Pat Neff had zero tolerance for lawbreakers in Mexia. *Library of Congress.*

H.C. Greathouse took his time devoting a full week to the assignment. The secret agent's shocking report "was of such a nature that it was hard to believe" Barton informed the governor, causing the two to agree they needed a second opinion. Greathouse returned to Mexia in the company of a federal agent. Their joint finding, Barton told Neff, was "even worse than the one submitted by Greathouse to begin with."

As Neff well knew, martial law and National Guard occupation rubbed most Texans the wrong way if such drastic action was not taken as the last resort only after all other remedies had proved ineffective. The Rangers, as usual, were confident they could handle the situation in Mexia on their own. The governor had his doubts, but he was willing to let them try under two conditions: they would concentrate on the Winter Garden and Chicken Farm with the Adjutant General and Assistant Attorney General Clifford Stone riding shotgun. Although it went against the Rangers' grain to limit the scope of their clean-up and, worse yet, to have someone looking over their shoulder, they reluctantly agreed to Neff's conditions.

Two companies of Texas Rangers caught the clubs completely by surprise with simultaneous raids on January 7, 1922, which happened to be a busy Saturday night. Fortunately for all concerned, the armed guards at both locations offered no resistance and admitted the khaki callers into the inner sanctum of both establishments. Besides gambling equipment, six hundred quarts of whiskey and a substantial stash of narcotics, the raiders confiscated "a virtual arsenal of weapons." That a mere twenty-two men were taken to jail could only have meant the customers and female employees were let go.

The number-two man in the Attorney General's Office summoned every official responsible for enforcing the law in Limestone and Freestone Counties to a meeting the following day at the Winter Garden. The district judge, district attorney, county attorneys, county judges and county sheriffs had the gall to play dumb, insisting they were unaware the two notorious nightspots even existed. Their denials were an insult to the intelligence of Clifford Stone and the governor and a clear indication that the powers-that-be were happy with the status quo.

Stone and Adjutant General Barton had every intention of giving the Rangers the time needed to sweep Mexia clean, but the roadblocks thrown in their way by local authorities sabotaged that option. Less than forty-eight hours after the Winter Garden meeting, the frustrated pair gave the governor their recommendation. The only remedy for what was ailing Mexia was a strong dose of martial law administered by the National Guard.

"The Rangers could not, under law, open court, take a complaint, or fix a bond," Neff wrote years later in defense of his decision. "It was up to me to turn the prisoners loose, and the houses back to the outlaws, or to declare martial law." And so he did, signing the declaration on January 11 and telling Brigadier General Jacob F. Wolters to get a move on.

Wolters, an ex-politician who attacked Woodrow Wilson as a "socialist" during a losing bid for the U.S. Senate, had earned a reputation as a hard-nosed and heavy-handed militarist during the six-week occupation of Galveston a year and a half earlier. To prove he had not changed his stripes, the general told the first newspaper reporter he could find: "Tell the police chiefs at Dallas, Fort Worth and Orange to expect a large number of visitors tomorrow. Most of the visitors will come in boxcars."

General Wolters reached Mexia on January 12, a day ahead of his troops. He came out of a briefing from Adjutant General Barton with General Order No. 1 that laid out the ground rules for the occupation. No firearms, no loitering and no crowds would be permitted. The thirteen Texas Rangers still in town would function as the police force with the Winter Garden serving as the detention center and Guardsmen as the jailers.

Texas National Guard General Jacob F. Wolters (far left) and his staff.
RGD0005F0756R-001, Houston Public Library, HMRC.

The troop train was met the next afternoon at the Mexia station by a curious crowd that did not utter a word. But from the safety of Dallas, the editor of the *Mexia Evening News* had a lot to say and the *Morning News* gave him a front-page platform to say it. Calling Neff's deployment of the National Guard "indefensible," he seethed: "If martial law is to be invoked to suppress a few bootleggers and gamblers in a community that by the nature of its industries draws the unemployed and undesirable from far and wide, then the theory of civil law enforcement as against military strength is in a bad way."

In Mexia, however, the elected leaders adopted a conciliatory tone. The acting mayor came close to rolling out the red carpet for General Wolters and his citizen soldiers: "Since the governor has declared martial law, the proper thing for us to do is to cooperate with the commanding officer here regardless of our own personal opinion and to help the military accomplish their work."

The Guard was settling in and Mexiaites were learning the dos and don'ts of daily life under martial law when disaster struck the evening after the troops hit town. An irate cook in a hole-in-the-wall café across the street from the telephone company kicked a temperamental kerosene stove, causing it to explode in a ball of fire. In no more than two minutes, according to eyewitnesses, the flames turned that side of the block into a raging inferno.

Telephone operator Estelle Simmons was climbing the stairs to the second-floor switchboard but was drawn to the sidewalk by the sound of the loud explosion and shouts of alarm. She watched as frantic car-owners pushed their parked vehicles away from the curb, leaving them in the middle of the street. A passerby paused to offer his condolences to the president of the bank that was burning to the ground before his very eyes. Jack Womack said with a shrug, "It can't be helped, and besides it's insured."

In no longer than it took for that short exchange, the gusty wind blew red-hot embers onto roofs in the next block. Those structures too proved to be a tinderbox as the flames swiftly devoured them one at a time.

Operator Simmons raced up the stairs to her assigned seat at the switchboard and joined her co-workers in placing emergency calls to every community in the area with a fire department. None of the women noticed the roof was on fire, until glowing cinders rained down on their heads and clothing. Every operator without exception stayed at her post and continued to call for help. If not for their heroic efforts, Groesbeck and Corsicana

BOOM BROUGHT A WORLD OF TROUBLE

"Prendergast-Smith & Co's state bank burning. Million and a half dollars timelocked in vault. Mexia on fire, night of Jan. 14, 1922." *DeGolyer Library, Southern Methodist University, Texas Postcards Collection.*

never would have known to send the firemen, trucks and equipment that kept Mexia from going up in smoke.

The Rangers must have drawn the short straw that catastrophic night because the unenviable task of crowd control fell to them instead of the Guard. With persistence and drawn sidearms the state lawmen pushed ten thousand spectators out of the center of town for their own safety and to curtail looting before it got totally out of hand.

The sun rose the next day on a scene out of the Great London Fire of 1666. All that was left of two city blocks in the heart of the downtown district were the smoking skeletons of a hundred businesses of every description. Insurance adjusters assessed the loss at half a million dollars, when the buck was worth thirteen times more than it is today. But the biggest and most important bright spot was the amazing fact that no one perished in the conflagration.

J.K. Hughes, the oilman with spunk and public spirit, and Jack Womack, the banker without a bank, took out a full-page, morale-booster of an ad in the *Evening News:*

> *Mexia's growth will be continuous and permanent if we make it so. The feverish pursuit of quick riches without thought of the future has blighted*

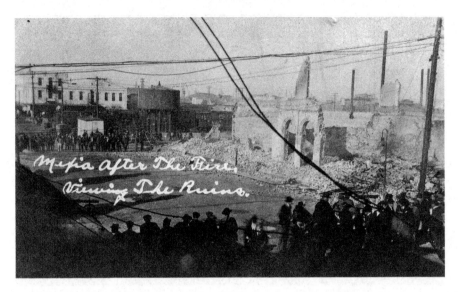

"Mexia after the fire. Viewing the ruins." Switchboard operators risked their lives to summon the firemen and equipment that saved the town. *DeGolyer Library, Southern Methodist University, Texas Postcards Collection.*

> *many a city similarly situated to Mexia. We can perpetuate our prosperity by investing a part of the vast wealth from the oil field in permanent improvements. Let us build the foundation of a great and modern city now, and the desirable citizens will come and remain.*

Dazed and discouraged townsfolk not only had to pull together and start rebuilding their devastated community but also had to endure an indefinite martial-law occupation that had barely begun. Although General Wolters would not make public the number of soldiers at his disposal, it was obvious he could have spared a few privates to lend a hand in the post-fire cleanup. That would have been the smart thing to do if for no other reason than it could have changed for the better the hostile attitude of many Mexiaites toward the Guard. But there is no evidence Wolters bothered to lift a finger to help or that the thought of doing so even crossed his mind. Instead, he announced four days after the fire that the military was assuming responsibility for sanitation and gave residents five days "to remove all rubbish and garbage from their property and the adjacent streets and alleys" or face arrest and a stiff fine.

BOOM BROUGHT A WORLD OF TROUBLE

The *Dallas Morning News* reported on January 17, "The rangers and soldiers are making a steady progress in rounding up the lawless element in the town and adjacent oil fields. About a dozen people are being arrested daily." Wolters confirmed eight days later the figure had increased to 263 with more busts to come.

Hundreds of "undesirables" had taken advantage of the "Sun-Down Order" issued by the general the night of the fire and left Mexia for parts unknown. Under Wolter's strict interpretation of the Texas vagrancy law, anyone without visible and legal means of support was subject to a speedy trial and, upon conviction—almost always the outcome—forced to pay a hefty fine or work off the punishment at a dollar a day. Without the petty crooks, prostitutes, gamblers and various villains to work the clip joints, the Juarez district shut down all because of the "Sun-Down" decree.

By the end of January, Wolters had good reason to believe law and order prevailed in Mexia and the rest of Limestone County. The criminal element was gone or in jail and their illegal enterprises eliminated. But the martial-law zone was still swimming in bootleg whiskey. It had to be coming from someplace else, and according to the reports that came across his desk, that source was a network of secret stills in the backwoods of Freestone County.

The Guard had a devil of time pinpointing the precise location of the moonshiners. The cedar brush and thickets were so dense in parts of Freestone County that a man could pass within spitting distance of a hidden still and never know it. The solution was to search from the air, a tactic never tried before in Texas. But the *Mexia Daily Telegraph* had an airplane and Wolters had a young lieutenant with a pilot's license. The intrepid aviator flew a series of reconnaissance missions with a pencil, pad of paper and map in his lap. In no time, he had the exact location of the majority of active stills.

However, for the National Guard to conduct raids in Freestone County, the governor had to expand the martial law zone to include Limestone's misbehaving neighbor. Neff was happy to oblige and went along with Wolter's request to delay his announcement until noon on February 3 in order to give the Guard and Rangers the jump on the unsuspecting moonshiners.

Rangers working undercover warned Wolters that resistance was likely in the Young Community, the center of whiskey-making. Putting their report in his own words, the general later wrote, "That portion of the community not actively involved in the violation of the law had knowledge of the operations and were in sympathy with the methods by which their neighbors made money."

After cutting the telephone lines into the area, the raiding party of Guardsmen and Rangers made their meticulously planned move at first light. They were welcomed with pot shots from the woods, "but a machine-gun trained here and there quickly silenced the sporadic firing" and prevented a pitched battle.

The invasion of Freestone County went on for hours with the troops and lawmen taking into custody every grown man unlucky enough to cross their path. Late that afternoon, fifty-nine prisoners were loaded into two trucks and three cars and driven to the county seat of Fairfield, where they were put on public display for the amusement of their friends and neighbors. The humiliating ritual was repeated at Teague before the detainees were delivered to the Winter Garden lockup at Mexia. And that was where they stayed, the innocent along with the guilty, for the next ten days.

In his official report, Wolters bragged about the stills destroyed (nine) and the gallons of whiskey (300) and mash (7,150) seized. But the loss of that trifling number of stills did not put much of a dent in the manufacture of moonshine in Freestone County nor justify the manpower and resources expended in the overreaching raid.

By February 15, Wolters must have run out of places to raid. Showing he had learned nothing from his controversial and illegal attempt to muzzle the editor of a Houston newspaper during the occupation of Galveston, the general had his troops storm a domino parlor on Mexia's main street a few doors down from the military headquarters. Seventy-two men, most of them retirement age, were lined up against the wall and dragged off to jail. Wolters defended the rash and ill-advised action with his final "General Order" that proclaimed, "Playing dominoes or loitering in domino parlors within the military district will be deemed prima facie evidence that the persons are vagrants."

While Governor Neff did not reprimand Wolters for the ridiculous raid, the statewide criticism may have motivated him to speed up his timetable for ending the military occupation. Four days after the domino parlor fiasco, he spoke to six hundred citizens of Limestone County at the opera house in Mexia. "I make no apology for sending the Rangers to this region or for declaring martial law. But now after six weeks what is to be done? This situation cannot go on forever." He concluded by asking for those in attendance who believed local and county officers could at last be trusted to enforce the law to raise their hands. Receiving the affirmative answer he was looking for, Neff spent the rest of the day overseeing preparations for the transfer of power.

BOOM BROUGHT A WORLD OF TROUBLE

Martial law ended in Limestone and Freestone Counties on March 1, 1922. After forty-seven days in Mexia, the National Guardsmen boarded the train for the trip home and to the families they had not seen in nearly two months. As for General Jacob Wolters, after relinquishing control of the occupied town to the ten thousand inhabitants who had stuck around, he followed his weary soldiers onto the train secure in the knowledge that another governor would have need of his special services in the near future.

Thanks to Mexia, oil production in the Lone Star State jumped 12 percent in 1922. Output for the overall field, which ran along a fault as far south as Luling, peaked in 1924 before dropping like a rock the rest of the decade. The population of Mexia gradually declined right along with the flow of crude before bottoming out in the range of six thousand in the early 1930s.

To many residents of Mexia, who rode out the roller-coaster boom, Colonel Albert E. Humphreys was a wealthy tycoon who truly cared about their town. When he was implicated in the Teapot Dome Scandal, they assumed their former benefactor would land on his feet as he always had. So it was with shock and sadness that Mexiaites read about his sudden death in May 1927. Humphreys was cleaning a shotgun in the gunroom of his mansion in Denver, Colorado, when the weapon accidentally discharged, killing him instantly. While that was the official version of the tragic event, it sounded like the Colonel must have been in far worse trouble than he ever let on and chose suicide over prison.

4

BAD OLD DAYS IN
BLOODY BORGER

Let's sing a song of Borger
Famed for its graft and rot
It's just a wide place in the wood,
This town that God forgot,
For this village large boasts deeper sin,
Than Sodom ever knew;
Come lend an ear, kind stranger,
And I'll whisper them to you.

Even stay-at-home Yankees who have never have ventured west of New England will recognize the iconic shape of the Lone Star State. When asked to identify the Panhandle, they usually succeed in pointing to the northernmost extremity that sticks out like an iron skillet.

Twenty-six square counties arranged in five neat rows make up the Panhandle. In terms of geography, history and culture, it has always been the most isolated section of Texas, a world unto itself, sharing more in common with eastern New Mexico and western Oklahoma than with the rest of the sprawling state.

Well into the third decade of the twentieth century, the Panhandle was cattle country with many more inhabitants walking around on four feet than on two. Amarillo, the only town of any size, counted a mere 15,494 heads in the census of 1920 but still dwarfed a scattering of smaller communities with populations below 2,000.

Oil came to the Panhandle in stages over eight long and drawn-out years of exploration on a shoestring budget. In 1918, a group of Amarillo businessmen, eager to imitate the instant millionaires in the eastern half of Texas, contacted a geology professor at the University of Oklahoma who had studied the underground formations in the Panhandle at the turn of the century. Even though he had been searching for water at the time, the geologist did recall an area along the Canadian River north of Amarillo that looked promising for natural gas and possibly oil.

Drilling on the businessmen's dime, the professor found gas nine out of ten times. However, oil proved more elusive, and the first producing well was not drilled until 1923. The number increased to sixteen the next year and fifty-six by the end of 1925, but that did not constitute a boom by Lone Star standards.

———•———

Halfway across the state of Oklahoma, Asa Phillip Borger could smell opportunity in the Texas Panhandle. The Missouri-born real estate promoter whom everyone called "Ace," maybe because he always seemed to have one up his sleeve, had made a fortune in the past decade and a half by creating start-up communities from nothing and by giving a new lease on life to dying towns. At twenty-seven, Borger was doing right well for himself with a lumberyard in his birthplace of Carthage, Missouri, but wanted more out of life—a whole lot more. So in 1915, Ace talked his brother Pete into having a go at the real estate game in Pilcher, the center of lead and zinc mining in eastern Oklahoma. The amateurs turned a modest profit in their maiden attempt at land hawking, but the money and experience were nothing compared to their partnership with the "King of the Wildcatters."

Tom Slick Sr. was the first of a long line of oil prospectors to have that title temporarily bestowed on him. Certain a huge pool of black gold was hiding beneath the Indian reservations of Oklahoma, the Pennsylvanian was unfazed by a discouraging series of dry holes. Then he struck pay dirt in March 1912 with the discovery of the largest oil field to date in the Sooner State.

Slick died of natural causes in 1930 and left $15 million apiece to his daughter and his fourteen-year-old namesake. Tom Jr. was a "Renaissance man" who did everything from founding the Scientific Research Institute in San Antonio and endowing the Tom Slick Professorship of World Peace at the University of Texas to searching for the Yeti in the Himalayas. As different as daylight and dark, the father and son had one tragic thing in common: both died in their forty-seventh year, with Tom Jr. perishing in a Montana plane crash.

BAD OLD DAYS IN BLOODY BORGER

The Borger boys teamed up with Tom Sr. in 1917 to pull a boomtown out of thin air. The wildcatter had struck it rich again, this time between Tulsa and Bristow, and needed a pair of able hands to build the necessary infrastructure from the ground up. Under Slick's tutelage, Ace and Pete learned how to buy land on the cheap, divide it into town lots, sell the lots for a sky-is-the-limit price, organize and staff a local government under their absolute control and satisfy the wants and needs of the people who flocked to the new speck on the map.

The Borgers and Slick Sr. soon parted company, presumably on good terms and all three with fatter wallets. Ace, with Pete in his role of low-profile junior partner, exploited the next big boom in the Greater Seminole Oil Field due east of Oklahoma City. This time, instead of conjuring up a town from scratch, they took the easier route of resurrecting a community with one foot in the grave.

The few remaining residents of Cromwell warmly welcomed the big-talking brothers. Without a clue how to capitalize on the once-in-a-lifetime windfall, they put their faith in the Borgers. In a matter of weeks, the comatose community was overrun by thousands of fortune-seekers, most looking for honest work but many others peddling female flesh and bootleg booze and enticing the gullible into unwinnable games of chance. Cromwell was soon known far and wide as "the most wicked city in the world."

Desperate to take their town back, the indigenous inhabitants talked a living legend of law enforcement into coming out of retirement. At the age of seventy, Bill Tilghman should have known better than to take the job of Cromwell marshal. As one of the fabled "Three Guardsmen," he had been credited with three hundred arrests, the killing of numerous outlaws who chose to shoot it out and the singlehanded capture of the notorious Bill Doolin. But that was three decades in the dim past, when the aged lawman was in his prime.

Tilghman survived a year in Cromwell on his wits and experience rather than his six-shooter, which gathered dust in his well-worn holster. His luck ran out on Halloween night 1924, when he was shot to death by a drunk Prohibition agent on the Borgers' take. Within the month, Bill Tilghman's friends and admirers avenged his murder by torching the town he could not tame.

Ace and Pete Borger did not stick around to watch Cromwell burn. They wisely made tracks before Tilghman was laid to rest.

On a crisp winter day in 1926, Ace saddled his horse for a close-up look at the next big oil boom that had everyone talking. Riding to the crest of the highest hill he could find, he surveyed the barren landscape down below. There was not a single tree or man-made edifice in sight, only a solitary derrick.

But that was what Ace Borger had ridden so far to see. Oil in the Texas Panhandle was neither a myth nor a mirage, and by seizing the moment, he could be in charge from the opening bell. Ace had learned from his mistakes in Cromwell, where the people who already lived there pressured him into sharing power and the spoils. In his mind, he had bent over backward to accommodate those nit-picking yokels only to have them turn on him.

This time Ace would take a page from Tom Slick's playbook by starting with a clean slate. And like Slick, he would give *his* town *his* name: Borger.

Ace moved with lightning speed. He paid a rancher $12,000 for 240 acres, filed the obligatory forms with the state and on March 8, 1926, opened the office of the Borger Townsite Company. He ran full-page advertisements in the Amarillo dailies and the small-town weeklies under the bold headline:

This was the oil well Asa "Ace" Borger rode from Oklahoma to see in 1926. *Legends of America.*

BAD OLD DAYS IN BLOODY BORGER

Finding a place to park was an everyday problem in Borger. *DeGolyer Library, Southern Methodist University, Texas Postcards Collection.*

"Your Opportunity Lies in Borger The New Town of The Plains." On Main and three other streets, 20- by 120-foot lots sold for $1,500 with a down payment of $450. At the close of business opening day, the cash receipts totaled over $60,000. In six frenzied months, the Borger Townsite Company would clear a cool million on Ace's $12,000 in seed money.

No one can say for sure how many people ended up in Borger or when they got there. The *Handbook of Texas*, the recognized authority on all things Texan, states: "Within ninety days of its founding, sensational advertising and the lure of 'black gold' brought over 45,000 men and women to the new boomtown." Fantastic as it may sound today, that ballpark figure coincides with other educated guesses of the time. To put it in historical perspective, a population of 45,000 would have made Ace's Panhandle paradise the sixth-largest city in the Lone Star State in the mid-'20s behind only Dallas, El Paso, Fort Worth, Houston and San Antonio.

Borger found a place for his cronies from Cromwell. John R. Miller, his personal attorney and trouble shooter, filled the office of mayor in a sham election following incorporation in late October 1926. Miller in turn invited "Two Gun" Dick Herwig to establish his own corrupt and ruthless brand of law enforcement with "officers," to use the term loosely, of his own choosing. To keep the roughnecks and the rest of the oilfield labor force entertained and broke, Miller brought in Ma and Pa Murphy, two more Cromwell veterans with their obedient band of prostitutes.

Not even Ace Borger's most generous apologists can claim those personnel decisions were made without his knowledge and blessing. Miller was, after all, the founding father's right-hand man in place of Pete Borger, who inexplicably faded into the woodwork. (The younger brother lived to the ripe old age of ninety, dying just up the road at Stinnett in 1988.) While Ace publicly distanced himself from Herwig and the Murphys in order to maintain his carefully cultivated illusion of respectability, there can be no question that he personally profited from their criminal activities.

Dick Herwig was a convicted murderer who, rumor had it, bought his way out of a long prison term in Oklahoma. True or not, the fact remained that he spent less than a decade behind bars on a ninety-nine-year rap.

Herwig's moniker came from the pair of pearl-handle revolvers that appeared to be permanently attached to his hips. Pistol-whipping was one of his favorite pastimes, which the sadist practiced on defenseless victims whenever the mood struck him. For extra protection on his nightly rounds of the brothels and bars, Two-Gun took along a couple of vicious German shepherds. The trained attack dogs certainly came in handy considering the amount of money their master frequently carried. One thousand prostitutes paid eighteen dollars each and every week for the privilege of plying the oldest profession, a fee that in a six-month period exceeded half a million dollars.

The chief deputy or town marshal—Herwig went by both titles—was as clever as he was corrupt. His network of stills produced an endless supply of rotgut whiskey that twenty-four-hour saloons like the Rattlesnake Inn and Bloody Bucket were required to buy. In addition, he brewed a beer called "choc" due to its unpleasant chalky aftertaste. Herwig hired a chemist to conduct surprise tests of the liquor and beer that saloons and other establishments were serving, and anyone caught selling unofficial beverages was subject to a heavy fine or a bone-breaking beating.

Pleasure-seekers tired of sex and alcohol turned to myriad drugs, some illegal and some not, peddled on the street by dope pushers, in watering holes by barkeeps and behind store counters by pharmacists. Two-Gun Dick and his associates took a piece of this action, too, as well as that in the gambling dens and holes-in-the-wall that lined the dirt streets.

"Booger Town," as local smart-alecks referred to Ace Borger's pride and joy, went full blast through the end of 1926. Five hundred miles from Austin, the boomtown attracted about as much attention as the dark side of the moon in the state capitol. Miriam "Ma" Ferguson, wife of scandal-plagued "Farmer Jim" and the first woman elected governor of any state, was a live-and-let-live chief executive who pardoned two thousand Texans convicted under the state prohibition statute. She was not inclined to punish folks in faraway Borger, wherever that was, for letting their hair down.

For reasons that had nothing to do with the wild goings-on in the Panhandle, voters denied Mrs. Ferguson the traditional second term. As a Central Texas district attorney, Dan Moody had helped to turn the tide against the Ku Klux Klan with successful prosecutions of the nightriders for their cowardly crimes. Elected attorney general in 1924 at the age of thirty-one, Moody humiliated the incumbent and her impeached husband two years later in the Democratic runoff for the gubernatorial nomination, which was tantamount to victory in one-party Texas where Republicans were about as popular as horse thieves.

The wide-open boomtown in the Panhandle did not figure prominently in Dan Moody's bid for the Lone Star State's highest office nor did he put a

"Borger's First Birthday. March 8th [19]27." *DeGolyer Library, Southern Methodist University, Texas Postcards Collection.*

Retired ranger Frank Hamer (left) shows movie and television cowboy Roy Rogers the gun he used to kill fifty-one men and one woman, Bonnie Parker. *RGD0005F2521-001, Houston Public Library, HMRC.*

Borger housecleaning on his list of campaign promises. With much bigger fish to fry, the youngest governor in Texas history could have followed his predecessor's example and done nothing at all.

But that was not in Governor Moody's law-and-order nature. To allow the chaotic status quo to continue in Borger without at least trying to stamp out the organized crime and corruption was a distasteful option he could not stomach.

Moody had been in office less than three months when he sent Captain Frank Hamer of the Texas Rangers on an inspection tour of Borger. Two days later, on April 6, 1927, the future bushwhacker of Clyde Barrow and Bonnie Parker reported, "The worst crime ring I have seen in my 23 years as an officer exists in Borger." That was all the governor needed to hear. Moody dispatched eight Rangers under the joint command of Captains William W. Sterling and Tom Hickman to Borger with crystal-clear orders not to return "until the lawless unconditionally surrender."

BAD OLD DAYS IN BLOODY BORGER

On April 17, the day Sterling arrived, an inquisitive reporter asked how the legendary lawman planned on making the bad guys behave. He answered that the Rangers were "going to reverse the customary Borger procedure. Where the criminals have been killing officers, we are going to kill off some crooks." That rhetorical shot over the bow sent practically all of the gamblers, bootleggers, pimps, prostitutes and other parasites packing. In his description of the mass exodus, Captain Sterling wrote that the undesirables "were strung out along the highways in droves, some in cars and trucks, others afoot. Outbound trains, both passenger and freight, also did a land-office business."

Fearing the state cops would be coming for him, a safe bet under the circumstances, "Two-Gun" Dick Herwig skipped town with his ill-gotten gains. But he made two dumb mistakes. First, Herwig stopped far too soon—less than ten miles inside New Mexico. Second, he bought a roadhouse and thumbed his nose at Lone Star authorities with a giant sign that declared: "Eight Miles From Texas Rangers."

If he had not hailed from Oklahoma, Two-Gun would have understood the Rangers were not about to take a public insult like that lying down. Just when Herwig thought he had seen the last of the khaki-clad Texans, an entire company walked through the swinging doors of his highway saloon. Captain Bud Wright had gone to the trouble of securing special commissions for himself and his men as "dollar-a-year" federal agents. The Borger alumnus watched in open-mouth astonishment as the Rangers padlocked the place and ordered him to hit the road. Dick Herwig was free to go anywhere he wanted except Texas. He meekly obliged and never showed his face again in the Lone Star State.

Meanwhile in Borger, the Rangers, backed by a beefed-up contingent of U.S. marshals and Prohibition agents, dismantled the criminal infrastructure piece by piece. Two dozen bars and gambling joints were shut down tighter than a drum, a river of illegal spirits was seized and dumped in the nearest gutter and the stills that produced Herwig's official whiskey and beer were destroyed. Several hundred federal offenders were rounded up and marched to a domino parlor where they were given the choice of Leavenworth or voluntary relocation. Their duty done, the feds left town and the Rangers in charge, and at the end of the month—April 1927—they proclaimed Borger to be "100 percent better."

As a rule, the Texas Rangers were sharply critical of local law enforcement. Even on those occasions when the police and sheriff were honest and aboveboard, the Rangers felt they rarely measured up to their own high standards.

However, prior to the decontamination of Borger, the Rangers encountered a police chief they came to accept as an equal. The Ranger trio assigned to the northern Panhandle needed canine assistance in tracking down the killer of the wife of a gas station owner, and the closest bloodhounds belonged to the police chief at Plainview, 125 miles to the south. H.H. Murray was happy to lend a hand, or in this case a paw, and drove to Borger the next day—January 16, 1927—with his three dogs.

The bloodhounds picked up the suspects' scent but lost it in the derrick-covered countryside. The case grew cold, causing the Rangers and the Plainview policeman to reluctantly go their separate ways.

No one could have blamed Chief Murray for forgetting all about the unsolved homicide. Borger was miles out of his jurisdiction, and there was no shortage of cases for him to crack back home. But the coldblooded killing of a woman stuck in his craw, especially since he knew from experience that neither the Hutchinson County sheriff nor the Borger police department would do a thing to bring her murderer to justice.

Two months passed without a glimmer of hope. In fact, the hunt for the killers lost ground after the Borger cops misplaced the only hard evidence, the two bullets removed from the victim's body. The dejected chief was on the verge of throwing in the towel, when a trusted informant tipped him off to the identity and whereabouts of the triggerman.

Murray jumped in his cruiser, drove like a demon to Borger and arrested Scotty Hyden in his hotel room. He dragged his handcuffed prisoner kicking and screaming to the city jail and handed over the well-known bank robber with the full knowledge "that the moment my back was turned he would buy himself out."

The chief waited down the street to foil the staged "escape," which would give him the legal grounds to take Hyden to a real jail that did not have a revolving door. Less than half an hour after the booking, Murray saw his former prisoner running down the street with two cops huffing and puffing in phony pursuit. They even fired a few rounds to make it look good, but the visiting lawman could not help but notice that every shot was aimed at the ground. Murray got his man for the second time that night and transported him to another county that did not have an open-door policy.

And that was how H.H. Murray earned the respect of the Texas Rangers. Like them, the Plainview chief of police did not have an ounce of quit in him.

———•———

The Rangers lingered for another month in Borger before notifying the governor in early June 1927 that their presence was no longer required. The boomtown was now on the straight and narrow, and they were confident it would stay that way.

Manuel T. Gonzaullas, who achieved the distinction of being the first Texas Ranger with a Spanish surname, strongly disagreed with that optimistic assessment. On loan to the Bureau of Prohibition, Gonzaullas found out that lower-profile members of what he called the "conspiracy and ring" still held important positions in the city and county governments. He went on to predict that left to their own devices those individuals would reinstate the worst excesses of the wide-open period.

"Lone Wolf," the nickname that made Gonzaullas famous, had it right. Those criminals, who stayed in town and waited out the Rangers, ended their law-abiding masquerade and sent word to departed colleagues that the coast was clear. In three short months, it was business as usual in bloody "Booger Town."

As far as Borger was concerned, Dan Moody felt he had done his part to lay the foundation for a stable society in which decent, hardworking families could live in peace and prosper. That was what he heard from the Rangers, legislators and the press, and who was he to disagree? He may not have created Utopia in the Panhandle, but he was only the governor of Texas, not God Almighty.

In the absence of outside watchdogs, some backsliding was to be expected. That was why Moody was not alarmed by intermittent complaints from irate residents that vice and violence had returned to Borger. What town in Texas did not have backrooms where grown men could wet their whistles, place a bet or pay for the company of a willing woman? In short, it was time for the inhabitants of Borger—the good, the bad and everybody in between—to grow up and solve their own problems like any other community.

When the Texas legislature created a new judicial district in the Panhandle in the fall of 1927, Moody picked an old classmate from his law school days at the University of Texas as district attorney. The governor warned Curtis Douglas up front that he had to be tough on the criminal element in Borger and made him swear he would stay on the wagon for the duration of his term.

But the weak-willed prosecutor failed miserably on both fronts. He got far too chummy with the corrupt politicians and police, along with the entire cast of underworld characters, and with no end to the free drinks, he rarely drew a sober breath.

By September 1928, the governor had had his fill even if his friend had not. Fortunately for Moody, a qualified candidate was waiting in the wings to replace the incompetent drunk the day he turned in his resignation. That day was September 13, 1928.

It did not take long for all parties on both sides of the law to realize the new district attorney was cut from a radically different cloth. John A. Holmes had prior experience as a Panhandle prosecutor and for the past year had been in private practice in Borger. The forty-two-year old attorney was a devoted family man with a wife and a young daughter. Much more important than his biography were two established facts: the new DA could not be bought, and he was immune to intimidation.

Thinking Holmes was too good to be true, the cynical crime lords put his squeaky clean reputation to the test. To their surprise, he turned down every bribe. Hoping to scare him into playing along, they utilized a variety of threats including the oft-repeated prophecy that he would not live long enough to finish his term. Faced with an honest and fearless man with the power to do them harm, they marked him for death.

The assassination of John Holmes made front-page news throughout the state of Texas and across the country. Newspapers that normally buried Panhandle datelines in the back pages, if they gave them any ink at all, broke the shocking story with banner headlines: "Borger Prosecutor Shot And Killed," *Waxahachie Daily Light*; "Police Seek Clue in Borger Killing," *Brownsville Herald*; "Concealed Slayer Shoots Down District Attorney at Borger in His Yard," *Waco News-Tribune*.

The dedicated DA had worked late into the evening on September 13, 1929—the first anniversary of his appointment—preparing cases for presentation the next morning to a grand jury at Stinnett, the county seat. A few ticks after ten o'clock, he turned into the driveway of his stucco house and coasted into the one-car garage. Seconds later, he stepped out into the moonlight and closed the garage doors.

The lone assassin, who had waited patiently since sunset, took aim with a .38-caliber pistol from his hiding place in a clump of thick bushes. He fired five rounds in rapid succession, grazing Holmes's chest with the first, penetrating his rib cage on the right side with the second and hitting him in the back of the neck with the third. A rush of adrenalin must have caused the gunman to miss completely on the fourth and fifth attempts, but it did not matter.

Jumping out of the bushes, the killer calmly checked the bullet-riddled body for signs of life. Finding none, he rifled through the pockets of the dead man's coat for any incriminating papers until interrupted by the screams of the woman he had just turned into a widow. He scrambled over a fence and sprinted down the alley before anyone could get a good look at him.

Dan Moody reacted with cold fury to news of the murder of John Holmes, denouncing it as "a dastardly crime of a low-life assassin" and "one of the worst crimes ever committed in Texas." No less enraged was

the federal judge who presided over the Panhandle. In a speech to Amarillo business leaders shortly after the slaying, Judge James C. Wilson said, "In my opinion, the murder of Johnny Holmes was the most serious crime in the history of Texas in 30 years, and I believe the hand that fired the shot either was the hand of an official or had official sanction."

At the governor's behest, Hamer and Hickman, the Ranger captains intimately familiar with Borger, made a whirlwind return trip to the boomtown they thought they had tamed. It was clear to them after a couple of days in "Booger Town" the situation had deteriorated so much over the past two years that it was impossible to tell the Rangers had ever been there at all. In his written report to Moody, which

Governor Dan Moody was prepared to wash his hands of "Bloody Borger" until the assassination of the crime-fighting DA forced him to declare martial law. *RGD0005F0656A-001, Houston Public Library, HMRC.*

was leaked to the press, Hamer contended Borger had "the worst bit of organized crime" he ever had seen.

The Borger chief of police held a press conference for the sole purpose of calling Hamer a liar. The *Borger Daily Herald*, in an editorial challenge issued on the front page, told the lawman to put up or shut up: "Borger people are anxious for proof or disproof of the statement made by Ranger Captain Hamer to the effect that there exists here the 'worst bit of organized crime' he has ever encountered. If such a crime ring does exist here, Borger people demand the arrest of its leaders; if it does not exist, they demand a retraction."

In nearby Amarillo the *Daily News* chimed in with an editorial of its own that addressed the elephant in room: martial law. "While the gravity of the Borger situation, brought to a head by the murder of District Attorney Johnnie Holmes, is not to be minimized, there seems little justification for such a drastic measure as martial law." The editor then proceeded to contradict his caution against minimizing the wretched state of affairs: "Sending troops to Borger would give the city a black eye before the rest of the country that is undeserving. There have been numerous murders in Borger, and there have been ugly threats and allegations smacking of a conspiracy in lawlessness. But Borger's history is largely the history of every other oil field city."

The twisted logic of the Amarillo daily had been prompted by the September 25–26 visit of General Jacob F. Wolters, commander of the Texas National Guard. Before he placed Borger under martial law and sent in citizen-soldiers to occupy the town, Governor Moody wanted to see if Wolters was of the same mind.

In a clandestine meeting at an undisclosed location in Austin, General Wolters reported his findings in person to the governor. He made the case for military intervention, but stopped short of advocating it.

"You have given me the facts, but you have not volunteered any recommendations," an exasperated Moody said. "If you, having investigated the situation, were Governor of Texas, would you declare martial law?"

Backed into a corner, Wolters responded with a direct two-word answer: "I would."

Dan Moody nodded in agreement and obvious relief. The matter was settled, and the decision was made. The governor gave the general three days to get all his ducks in a row. The Guard would leave for Borger on Sunday, September 29.

BAD OLD DAYS IN BLOODY BORGER

As per the governor's instructions, preparations for the mobilization were made in strictest secrecy. For the mission, thirteen officers and eighty enlisted men, unmarried and with no dependents, were handpicked from the Guard units based in Dallas and Fort Worth. Dressed in civilian clothes, they were ordered to assemble at six o'clock Saturday evening at the Cow Town armory. The Guardsmen had no idea where they were going or why or for how long.

General Wolters would describe the events of the next day in his book *Martial Law and Its Administration* published the following year. Officers kept the men busy with drills until the midday mess. At two o'clock in the afternoon, a train with three Pullmans and a baggage car pulled onto the siding next to the armory.

The Guardsmen were called to attention for a few well-chosen, and hopefully illuminating, words from General Wolters. He told them, to the best of his recollection, "they were to entrain on the cars parked in their sight; they were going to an unnamed destination for an indefinite tour of duty; that their families and employers would on the following morning be notified."

Once the weekend warriors were in their seats and accounted for, the train made one more stop in the rail yard for freight cars containing two automobiles, three trucks and two ambulances. Then it was off to the Panhandle, but only a high-ranking handful of the passengers knew that for certain.

With nothing but time on their hands, the Guardsmen speculated on their destination. The sun in their eyes meant the train was headed west. Those who kept up with the news said that had to mean Borger, where someone had gunned down a prosecutor.

In those days, newsmen made a habit of hanging around train stations. Sometimes it yielded a scoop, as it did late that sleepy Sunday for a cub reporter in Wichita Falls. When the westbound train chugged into the station, two curious things caught his eye. First, the passenger cars were full of clean-cut young men without a woman in sight. Second, every one of them stayed in his seat instead of hustling onto the platform for a pack of cigarettes or a snack like ordinary travelers.

The excited young journalist ran to the nearest pay phone and filed his story. In a matter of minutes, the wire services hummed with the breaking news that a trainload of National Guardsmen had been sighted on a westerly course for the Panhandle.

In the capital, the press corralled the governor and gave him a chance to deny the report. When the interrogators refused to accept "no comment" for an answer, Moody conceded the cat was out of the bag with this good-natured quip: "Come around tomorrow, and I'll show you the proclamation."

The train rolled into Amarillo at four o'clock in the morning on Monday the thirtieth of September. The officers and men rubbed the sleep from their eyes and filed into the Santa Fe station, where a hearty breakfast was waiting. They ate their fill, changed into their uniforms and climbed back on the train.

At half past eight, the National Guard express pulled into Borger. In his stiff "just the facts, ma'am" style, General Wolters recorded the event for posterity: "I did not anticipate any hostile demonstrations and while a crowd of people had gathered at the station there was no demonstration one way or the other. The soldiers were detrained in an orderly manner on the side of each car, without word of command, with the rifle at port arms. Twenty-five paces in advance of each platoon were two selected men with riot shotguns at port arms."

The Guardsmen had been on the ground for no more than a minute when a drunk staggered up to one of them. Without a word or a verbal order from his superiors, the soldier made the first arrest of the occupation.

That was exactly the kind of first impression Wolters wanted to make. "This occurrence, in the presence of spectators, had a good psychological effect, however minor the incident was." The message was that the Guard meant business, and everyone who watched the unfortunate barfly be led away got it loud and clear.

Like a well-oiled machine, the Guard shifted into high gear. MPs took up positions at major intersections, as squads of three to five soldiers fanned out and began nonstop patrols of the town. City hall, police headquarters and the jail were under the complete control of the military by nine o'clock. Every official, from the mayor on down, was locked out of his office and physically removed from the premises. All members of the police force were relieved of duty, stripped of their badges and firearms and told to clear out.

Twelve miles away at Stinnett, the same scenario was playing out. The officer in charge informed the county sheriff and his deputies their services were longer needed and ordered them to leave their badges and weapons at the door. As the clock on the Hutchinson County courthouse struck ten, the lieutenant gave the compulsory public reading of the governor's martial law proclamation from the front steps.

On Tuesday, October 2, General Wolters named the nine members of the military Board of Inquiry, empowered to look under every rock for wrongdoers, first and foremost the party or parties responsible for the murder of DA Holmes. Three were Guard officers above the rank of captain and six were civilians; four were the personal picks of Governor Moody to replace local officeholders, including the slain district attorney, and the other two Ranger Captains Hamer and Hickman. The board did not beat around the bush but went straight to work, questioning eleven city and county officials in a grueling fourteen-hour session.

The Rangers and the rank-and-file Guard were busy, too. On October 2, in "the beginning of the actual cleanup," according to an Amarillo paper, "at least 36 saloons, blind tigers [speakeasies], gambling halls and houses of ill repute" were raided and presumably shut down. At the end of the following day, the number of raided establishments had risen to forty-five with one hundred persons of both sexes behind bars on a laundry list of charges.

The *Amarillo Daily News*, which had been dead-set against martial law before it was imposed, suddenly sang a different tune. The once critical editor praised "Borger's transition…into a peaceful community," marveling that the feat "has been accomplished by national guardsmen without mishap. Only two shots, both accidental, have been fired since martial law was declared last Monday. Khaki-clad patrolmen direct traffic without the ordinary back talk from motorists. Drinkers stay at home and lock the doors before imbibing."

A delegation of Borger's "best," citizens purporting to be upright pillars of the community, asked for a meeting with General Wolters on Saturday, October 5. They wanted to know what else had to happen for the state of martial law to be lifted.

Wolters's answer was clear and to the point: "The resignation of the sheriff and all of his deputies, the resignation of the two constables and their deputies, the resignation of the mayor and the commission, and all members of the police department, and the replacement of these officers by men satisfactory to District Attorney Clem Calhoun."

The general had laid his cards on the table, and now the marked men had to play the hand or fold. Most of the small fry dropped out almost immediately, turning in their resignations and quietly leaving town. But the bigger fish, like the mayor and sheriff, dug in their heels and refused to knuckle under. They blindly clung to the false hope that Wolters and Moody would blink first and permit them to remain in office at least until elections could be held. However, as the days went by and not the slightest chink appeared in the armor of the general or the governor, the holdouts themselves began to crack under mounting pressure from their families and cronies to be done with it.

Attorneys for the sheriff and mayor finally requested a private conference on October 14 with General Wolters and his staff, along with Governor Moody's appointees for judge and district attorney. The only thing holding up the two men's capitulation was their fear of prosecution for crimes committed while in office. Wolters gave them his word they were free to leave town as soon as he had their resignations on the table in front of him. Two minutes later, the last remaining obstacle to the end of martial law in Borger had been eliminated.

The mayor did not go quietly, however, and insisted upon playing the martyr to the bitter end. Repeating almost word for word the statement made by the state representative when he took his leave early in the occupation, the mayor whined, "Some man or men of necessity had to be the 'scapegoat' for the wrath of Dan Moody, and it so happened that I, among a few other officials, was chosen for the ordeal."

Martial law officially came to an end on the afternoon of October 18, 1929, with the long-awaited departure of the National Guard. There was no parade or public celebration other than a collective sigh of relief from the remaining residents, who, for the first time in the history of the boomtown, had control of their community.

General Wolters's one regret was that he left the murder of District Attorney John Holmes unsolved. It had not been for lack of trying. A Court of Inquiry had devoted many days to an exhaustive investigation of the crime and even narrowed down the lengthy list of suspects to five. But there was insufficient evidence for an indictment, much less a conviction, and the case never went to trial.

———•———

As for Ace Borger, the string-pulling town founder came out of the crackdown smelling like a rose. Acting as if nothing had happened, he went back to being Borger's business leader and political power broker. "How do you run a man out of town when he owns most of it?" was the question that stumped Ace's enemies. In the end, they had no choice but to tolerate his presence.

Everyone except Arthur Huey, the county tax collector, who hated Ace Borger with a passion only blood could quench. What evidently turned Huey's loathing into homicidal rage was Borger's refusal to bail the sticky-fingered taxman out of jail after his arrest on an embezzlement charge.

As part of his daily routine, Ace always went by the post office to pick up his mail. Huey knew that and was waiting from him on the last day of August 1934. Borger had his head down and was thumbing through the envelopes when he heard a familiar voice yell, "You son of a bitch, get your gun!"

Ace looked up to see Huey already had the drop on him. Before he could reach for his concealed pistol, the taxman fired two shots, hitting his nemesis in the body with both. Gravely wounded, Borger slumped to the floor, but his attacker kept on shooting until the smoking Colt .45 was empty. On the off chance his victim had a flicker of life left in him, the killer borrowed Ace's .44 from under his coat and finished him off with four rounds from his own gun.

Standing over the dead man, Huey was heard to say, "Well, you SOB, I got you this time!"

At his murder trial that December, Arthur Huey's lawyer tried his best to sell a plea of self-defense. To his surprise, as well as his client's, the jury found in favor of the defendant and acquitted him of the cold-blooded, premeditated killing. The not-guilty verdict mirrored public opinion in a community where the majority felt in their bones that Ace Borger, the greedy genius behind the boomtown nightmare, had it coming.

The history of Borger was written not in oil but blood and measured in coffins instead of barrels. Compared to other Texas booms in the first half of the twentieth century, Borger's did not amount to much and most definitely did not approach the scale of a Spindletop, a Ranger, a Desdemona or a Mexia. The fact that the town found a way to live with the past while forging a fresh future is more a tribute to the determination of its people than any gifts from nature.

5

Drowning in an Ocean of Oil

Columbus Marion Joiner must have been a likable old coot. For thirty years, the Alabaman, who spent a grand total of seven weeks in school, wandered back and forth across Texas, Oklahoma, Arkansas and Louisiana on the hunt for oil deposits but had always come up empty-handed. He made a living by convincing naïve farm folk, most of them widows, that he was "this close" to finding the pot at the end of the rainbow overflowing with the riches that had eluded them, and him, their whole hand-to-mouth lives. For a piddling amount of money or a place to sleep or a meal or whatever else they might be able afford, he could guarantee them a piece of his dream and theirs, too.

Joiner did not bother the trusting marks with the petty details, such as that he did not have the faintest idea what he was doing or that he had yet to find a single drop of oil. He oversold the shares of the occasional wells he drilled with the understanding that success would land him in prison for fraud. But that is what he was—a charming charlatan, better suited to the carnival circuit than legitimate business.

A.D. "Doc" Lloyd did an impressive impersonation of something he was not, a trained geologist. He talked "Dad"—Joiner's nickname now that he was showing his age—into believing his elusive El Dorado was waiting for him in the Piney Woods of East Texas. In reality, Joiner did not need much convincing. He was too old for the life on the road and ready to retire to a rocking chair on the front porch of a little cabin he could call his own. But that took money, and as usual, he had none.

"Henderson Texas gets oil fever." *DeGolyer Library, Southern Methodist University, Texas Postcards Collection.*

Lloyd got it into his head that Rusk County was the ideal spot to drill the well that would solve their problems. With nothing to lose but time, Joiner agreed to give it a shot. They drilled their initial well in 1927 with a rusty, third-hand rig that frequently fell apart. Like the farmers who bankrolled the undertaking, the crew had fallen under Dad's spell and put in long, backbreaking days for his pie-in-the-sky promises. After a succession of wells, Joiner had a hunch that Daisy Bradford's farm eight miles west of Henderson was the place his luck was destined to change.

Haroldson Lafayette Hunt, an Arkansas poker player turned oilman, heard that two oddball characters were drilling for crude in the one part of Texas every expert had scratched off his to-do list. But the instincts that would someday make him the richest man in America told him it was worth the price of a train ticket to see firsthand what was going on in Rusk County. When Hunt showed up, Joiner was sinking his third well on Mrs. Bradford's land. The smiling stranger unpacked a contraption that he said the inventor claimed could detect the presence of oil. His interest piqued, Joiner invited Hunt to try it out on his well. Whether the future billionaire revealed that the hole tested positive is not an established fact, but it turned out to be a moot question after the Daisy Bradford No. 3 struck oil on the evening of October 3, 1930.

No one had an inkling of the colossal scope of Dad Joiner's discovery. Months of trial-and-error exploration and painstaking mapmaking went into determining the exact dimensions of the East Texas field. It turned out to be the largest pool of oil ever found in the continental United States, covering 140,000 acres, or approximately 225 square miles, and all or part of five counties: Gregg, Rusk, Upshur, Smith and Cherokee.

For Joiner, the Daisy Bradford No. 3 was his worst nightmare come true. He had always wanted to hit it big but never *that* big. Every individual who had ever bought a piece of the old con artist's action demanded cash on the barrelhead—or else. To protect the interests of the army of mom-and-pop investors, a judge froze Joiner's assets and told the claimants to take a number. That was H.L.

This life-sized statue (top) in the museum at Kilgore was how H.L. Hunt wanted to be remembered. But this (right) is how the billionaire really looked. *East Texas Oil Museum, Library of Congress (top); RGD0005F6530-001, Houston Public Library, HMRC (right).*

Hunt's cue. First, he sent Dad packing with a check for $1 million. Second, he formulated a plan to provide creditors big and small with a "fair" return on their investment. Fairest of all, of course, was the bundle Hunt made on the court-sanctioned pay-off.

Dear old Dad rode off into the sunset and, for a time, basked in the glow of his East Texas triumph. But once a wheeler-dealer always a wheeler-dealer, which explains why Columbus Marion Joiner was insolvent the day he died in 1947.

The boom in East Texas was open to all comers because the major companies lacked the foresight to plant their flag in advance. Unlike Eastland County and, to a lesser extent, Mexia, most of the oil leases in the Piney Woods were up for grabs. For once, the small independents, the "wildcatters," had a fighting chance.

Neither big nor small but somewhere in between, two boyhood friends from Athens hit the ground running early in the East Texas oil rush. Clint Murchison and Sid Richardson would do all right for themselves, as they always did.

Murchison gave Trinity University the good old college try but did not last the semester. Caught shooting craps, the defiant freshman quit school rather than sign a no-gambling pledge. He toiled as a teller in his dad's bank until the day a bank examiner insisted upon a strict accounting of his till.

A lay-off a few years earlier had put sixteen-year-old Richardson on the road to riches. Losing a dollar-a-day job at the cotton compress, he hitched a ride to Louisiana and found his true calling. His impersonation of a down-on-his-luck city slicker elicited so much sympathy from Pelican State farmers that they practically gave him their prize calves. With the $3,500 profit from the sale of the charitable contributions, he was able to afford a year and a half of higher education.

While Murchison was making the world safe for democracy in the First World War, Richardson made his first killing in the Lone Star oilfields. He could not resist flaunting his newfound wealth by rolling into Athens behind the wheel of a shiny new Cadillac. As he fondly recalled decades later, "When I left, all those guys sitting on those benches around the square jumped up and followed me right out of town."

Eager to show his best buddy how it was done, Richardson whisked the cynical veteran off to the Burkburnett field within days of his discharge. When it took just twenty-four hours of buying and selling oil leases to quadruple their $50,000 grubstake, Murchison was hooked. Each launched his own drilling company, and by the mid-'20s the two wildcatters were filthy rich. Confident he could live comfortably on $5 million for the rest of his life, Murchison bowed out of the oil business at the tender age of thirty. But he jumped back in the game in 1927 to take his mind off the tragic loss of his wife to jaundice.

The fabulous East Texas boom cut both ways for Richardson, Murchison and many of their contemporaries. Richardson made money hand over fist until Piney Woods crude glutted the market in 1931, dropping the price to pennies a barrel. Looking back on those crazy times, he later said, "I had a monthly income of $25,000. Six months later, my income was $1,600 a month, and the bank was taking it all as payment on the $250,000 I owed. But by March 1932, the price of oil was up again. I had four ten-dollar bills and was ready to go." And go he did, opening the Keystone Field in Far West Texas in 1935. Richardson not only kept his head above water but also became, according to an inside source at Chase Manhattan Bank, the first billionaire west of the Mississippi.

Murchison was never far behind, though how far he refused to say. Annoyed by nosy questions about the size of his personal fortune, he snapped, "After the first hundred million, what the hell!" He spread his risk after World War II by expanding his interests beyond the oil patch. He bought a New York publishing house in the belief the baby boom was bound to increase the demand for textbooks. Anticipating a workforce with more leisure time, he purchased *Field & Stream* and a fishing tackle manufacturer. By the middle of the 1950s, the Murchison empire encompassed forty-eight companies with fifty thousand employees.

The key to his success was a keep-it-simple philosophy, something a subordinate learned on an errand to Mississippi. He

Clint Murchison Sr. jumped back in the oil game just in time for East Texas boom. *Murchison family and DeGolyer Library, Southern Methodist University.*

Glenn McCarthy (right) and his pilot give Miss Texas a boost. The wildest wildcatter of them all was Edna Ferber's inspiration for the character Jett Rink in her novel *Giant*. *RGD0005F6354R-002, Houston Public Library, HMRC.*

called Murchison in his Dallas office to suggest there may have been more to the acquisition of an insurance company than at first met his eye. "There's nothing complicated about it," barked the straightforward tycoon. "A hundred thousand shares at $105. That's $10.5 million, a simple business deal."

Sid Richardson feared the loneliness of retirement and vowed, "I'll still be trading when they bury me." He did stay busy until the end, dying in his sleep on his private island five miles off Rockport in 1959. Clint Murchison, however, learned how to relax in his twilight years. Prior to his passing in 1968, he ran a country store in his hometown and studied the comings and goings of migratory birds.

East Texas had its share of unruly boomtowns but none to rival Borger and Mexia or Ranger on its calmest day. Kilgore might have made that list had it not been for the preemptive action taken by the Texas Rangers.

The five hundred inhabitants of the serene hamlet that straddled the Rusk-Gregg County line rubbed their eyes in disbelief shortly after sunrise on December 29, 1930. During the night, a horde of crude-crazed outsiders had invaded the peaceful community looking for their share of the black gold discovered earlier in the week. Of the ten thousand fortune hunters who transformed Kilgore into an anything-goes boomtown, hundreds were professional predators. The one local lawman and the shorthanded sheriff were no match for the con men and cutthroats, muggers and madams, bootleggers and bandits who took over the defenseless town.

Two Rangers—M.T. "Lone Wolf" Gonzaullas and his partner, J.P. Huddleston—put in an appearance on February 2, 1931, and immediately served notice on the outlaw element. "Crime may expect no quarter in Kilgore," declared Gonzaullas. "Gambling houses, slot machines, whiskey rings and dope peddlers might as well save the trouble of opening because they will not be tolerated in any degree." Shady characters were given the choice of beating a hasty retreat or going straight to jail. Since the local calaboose could only accommodate a handful of guests, Gonzaullas set up a "trotline" in the middle of town. He tightly secured a long logging chain to several sturdy sycamores and attached small sections of forged metal that kept detainees on a short leash. Male prisoners wore heavy chain collars padlocked at the base of the skull, while females were shackled at the ankle in deference to their sex.

Gonzaullas subsequently took pity on the pathetic prisoners, who were exposed to subfreezing temperatures and the indignity of relieving themselves in public. The infamous trotline was moved inside an abandoned church, where shotgun guards stood watch night and day. At this point, most captives were ready to hit the highway in exchange for their freedom. Those charged with minor offenses were turned loose on the condition they never show their faces again in Kilgore.

Gonzaullas and Huddleston compiled a long list of undesirables, many more than the two Rangers could hope to handle. Secretly summoned reinforcements came to Kilgore on the afternoon of March 2, and by sundown, more than four hundred suspects were cooling their heels in the converted church. Although the mass arrests turned the tide, "Lone Wolf" Gonzaullas stayed in the trouble spot through the summer. He had his hands full raiding gambling dens, closing backroom bars and encouraging prostitutes to take their oldest profession somewhere else.

A retired Ranger reminisced years later about the tough tactics employed in the Kilgore crackdown. "We simply didn't have the time, or the facilities, to arrest a hundred or more men a day, lock them up and then spend days in the courtroom until they came to trial. There were simply too many of them and too few of us." He paused thoughtfully before continuing. "We stopped crime the only way you can stop it—with whatever force is necessary. At times, a warning to leave town was enough. Some of the really tough ones wanted to argue the finer points of the situation. Them we shot."

The Texas Rangers were not the only hard-as-nails lawmen in the bare-knuckle boomtown. Kilgore's top cop had his own well-deserved reputation for taking swift and drastic measures. Recognizing two newcomers as recently paroled robbers he personally sent up the river, the police chief sternly warned them not to linger overnight in Kilgore. When the ex-cons nodded and went on their way, he presumed the matter was closed.

Returning the next day from a nearby town, the chief spied the two hijackers driving past the railroad yard. He spun around, gave chase and quickly caught up with them. Hitting the brakes and grabbing his rifle, he jumped out of the patrol car and put a bullet through the neck of the driver. With a dead man at the wheel, the vehicle careened out of control and crashed into a boxcar. A second shot ended the passenger's escape but spared his life.

The sharpshooting cop was handcuffing the wounded survivor, when his excited subordinates skidded to a stop. A winded patrolman asked in amazement, "How did you know those fellows just robbed a grocery store? We thought you were in Longview!"

"What robbery? I don't know beans from corn about any robbery," the chief answered. "I warned these two yesterday to get out of town, and they didn't take me seriously!"

Kilgore was soon known far and wide not as a place to avoid after dark but for the "World's Richest Acre," the greatest concentration of oil wells on the planet. One thousand derricks in the center of town were a source of pride for the pacified community and, for quite a while, something of a tourist attraction.

Governor Ross Sterling monitored the efficient cleanup of Kilgore for lessons he could apply to a law-enforcement challenge on a much larger scale. Independent oilmen throughout East Texas were in open revolt against state regulation of excessive production, and the Rangers did not have the numbers to compel the "wildcatters" to back down.

Sterling had campaigned for governor as "the fat boy from Buffalo Bayou." The 265-pound multimillionaire poked fun at his gigantic girth to divert attention from his even bigger bank account. He also never tired of reminding voters that he started out as a dirt-poor farm boy in Chambers County who had to quit school at thirteen to lend his widowed father a full-time hand with his twelve siblings. Sterling's meteoric rags-to-riches rise began in 1903 at Sour Lake, where he sold everything under the hot Texas sun to the workers in the Hardin County oilfield. Within a decade, he was the founding president of Humble Oil Company and on his way to amassing a fortune worth an estimated $50 million.

Selling his oil interests in 1925, Sterling plowed his profits back into real estate and publishing in his adopted hometown of Houston. He merged the *Post* and the *Dispatch* into a single daily and hired former governor William P. Hobby to ride herd on the newspaper.

Sterling entered the 1930 race for governor against the advice of friends, who argued that his wealth would alienate an electorate hard hit by the deepening Depression. Although he trailed Miriam "Ma" Ferguson, stand-in for impeached husband Jim, by seventy-two thousand votes with barely 20 percent of the ballots in the Democratic primary, an anti-Ferguson avalanche carried him to victory in the runoff.

The affable amateur could not have chosen a worse time to rule the roost in the Lone Star State. Like the clueless occupant of the White House,

Sterling was blamed for the dead-in-the-water economy, the disappearance of thousands of jobs and the absence of a "safety net" to keep the unemployed from falling through the cracks. He was, in short, the Herbert Hoover of Texas.

The new and untested governor had no sooner taken the oath in January 1931 than he faced a serious crisis in East Texas. Ignoring a toothless decree from the Railroad Commission to slow down, independent operators pumped around the clock, filling as many as half a million barrels a day. As the price of crude plunged to six cents a barrel, they increased production to make up the difference.

While the wildcatter believed in his God-given right to do as he pleased regardless of the impact on the market, he often had no other alternative. With the bank breathing down his neck, the oil-patch entrepreneur could not afford to wait for the price to rebound. The small independent had an ally in the Texas motorist, whose sole concern was what the corner station charged him for a tank of gas. If overproduction kept the cost of the essential fuel at seven cents a gallon, then he was all for overproduction. On the other side of the barricade was Big Oil, which demanded a government crackdown on the wildcatters. Since the governor came from the same background, the major companies assumed he shared their concern for plummeting prices.

But Sterling feared the political consequences of showing favoritism toward the oil lobby and passed the buck by calling the state legislature into special session. Even after lawmakers failed to address the thorny issue, he refused to rein in the maverick independents. However, when daily production exceeded one million barrels, the governor did an abrupt about-face. Over the objections of his closest advisors, including ex-governor Dan Moody, he decided to send in the National Guard.

To avoid a public relations problem, Sterling made a monumental mistake. Instead of Adjutant General William W. Sterling, the logical choice to lead the East Texas mission, he put General Jacob F. Wolters in charge. While it was possible that Sterling's last name may have caused confusion, Wolters's day job as general counsel for Texaco proved to be a far more serious liability.

At six o'clock on the morning of August 17, 1931, the moment the martial law decree took affect, Wolters commandeered the Kilgore city hall as his headquarters. Never known for his tact, he gave the assembled oilmen until nightfall the next day to halt production, or "it's jail for those who haven't quit." Ninety-nine officers and 1,104 enlisted men of the Texas National Guard occupied the counties of Upshur, Gregg, Rusk and Smith. Under their watchful eye, the oil tap was turned off right on schedule. Despite ominous predictions that the unpopular invasion would meet with widespread violence, the citizen-soldiers encountered surprisingly little resistance. Except for trading shots with a speeding car and ferreting out adolescent arsonists responsible for a rash of fires in Kilgore, Guardsmen complained East Texas was dull duty compared to their previous deployments in Mexia and Borger.

For most, the boredom was short-lived. One-third of the contingent was sent home on August 25 in advance of the second phase of the operation, enforcement of the production quota set by the Railroad Commission. A few days later, a more drastic reduction left a token force of 120 Guardsmen to patrol the oilfield.

Governor Sterling soon learned that his most formidable foe was the federal court, which granted a temporary injunction in October 1931 that permitted the majority of independents to pump all the oil they desired. After a special three-judge panel made the injunction permanent four months later, martial law was nothing more than an expensive exercise in futility. Infuriated by what he considered federal interference in the internal affairs of a sovereign state, Sterling stuck to his empty guns. Meanwhile,

Judging from the expressions on the faces of Ross Sterling and his family, this picture may have been taken after he lost his bid for a second term. *RGD0005F0699-0002, Houston Public Library, HMRC.*

General Wolters lost interest and relinquished his command to return to private life.

Ruling that Governor Sterling's original martial law decree was constitutionally flawed, the U.S. Supreme Court upheld the permanent injunction on December 12, 1932. Nine days later, the last National Guardsmen pulled out of East Texas.

When it was all said and done, the oil industry in the Lone Star State wound up worse off because in the spring of 1933, Piney Woods crude was selling for four cents a barrel. As for Ross Sterling, he was already long gone after becoming only the third governor in fifty-nine years to be denied an automatic second term by dissatisfied voters.

———•———

As the Depression tightened its stranglehold on the country, East Texas was an oasis of prosperity due to "Doc" Joiner's incredible discovery. In Rusk County, twenty-five miles east of Tyler, a bustling beehive called New London leaped to life and inside a month boasted a score of businesses and a population of six hundred.

Petroleum proceeds paid for a modern junior-senior high school, a million-dollar complex that proud residents bragged was the finest rural educational facility in the nation. Children were bused from miles around to classes at the New London school.

At three o'clock on the afternoon of Thursday, March 18, 1937, most of the five hundred pupils, from fifth graders to high school seniors, assembled in the auditorium. Another ninety-five attended a study hall in an adjoining wing while small groups were scattered throughout the sprawling structure. One hundred yards away in the gymnasium, a PTA meeting was coming to order.

It took next to nothing to ignite the natural gas that had accumulated beneath the main building. Possibly an electric switch shorted out or maybe a sanding machine in the shop was the source of the fatal spark. No one could ever say for certain. Without warning, the volatile gas exploded. Erupting through the floor, the devastating force of the bomb-like blast blew out the walls. Robbed of support, the roof came crashing down on the helpless victims, burying them under tons of rubble.

Mothers from the parent-teacher gathering, administrative personnel and townspeople reached the doomsday scene in seconds. The entire front section of the central building, which contained the crowded auditorium, lay

New London the day after the deadliest school disaster in American history. *MSS0334-1277, Houston Public Library, HMRC.*

in twisted ruin. Littered with random wreckage and a score of tiny bodies, the schoolyard resembled a war-torn battle zone. The anguished cries of hysterical mothers pierced the dusty air. Overwhelmed by the sheer horror of the catastrophe, the district superintendent staggered through the debris in a daze screaming, "My God! Those poor children!"

Roughnecks from the nearby oilfield quickly started the desperate search for survivors. Aided by giant cranes and floodlights, two thousand rescue workers labored through the night with torn and bloody hands to remove the dead and injured. Praying their children might be among the pitifully few found alive, numb parents maintained a grim vigil. By dawn, the death toll had reached two hundred with no end in sight.

Next of kin wandered the countryside checking hospitals for their sons and daughters. The painful quest was slowed to a crawl by the morbidly curious, who clogged the highways for a glimpse of the devastation. Martial law was imposed, and the National Guard finally cleared the roads.

At Overton, five miles from the disaster, a skating rink was turned into a temporary morgue. Grief-stricken families filed past rows of bloodstained sheets as nurses lifted the shrouds for identification of the dead. Heartbreaking moans meant another missing child had been found.

SINCLAIR NO.1 COLE
NEAR GLADEWATER. MOST DISASTEROUS
FIRE IN TEXAS OIL HISTORY. TAKING
9 LIVES WITH BUT A MOMENTS NOTICE.
166

"Sinclair No. 1 Cole near Gladewater. Most disasterous [*sic*] fire in Texas oil history. Taking 9 lives with but a moment's notice." *DeGolyer Library, Southern Methodist University, Texas Postcards Collection.*

For those who got out alive, blind luck or fast thinking made all the difference in the world. A thirteen-year-old boy picked that day to play hooky because he feared a birthday paddling from his schoolmates. As the walls buckled, the study hall teacher ordered her charges to take cover under their desks. Unbelievably, all escaped death, including the sole survivor of the varsity football team.

The funerals began at New London and surrounding communities the day after the explosion. As dozens of victims, the offspring of oilfield gypsies, were laid to rest in thirty-four Texas counties, the enormous scope of the calamity hit home across the Lone Star State.

Five days after the tragedy, a military court of inquiry released the findings of a rushed investigation. The verdict revealed that a chain reaction of human errors instead of criminal misconduct was responsible for the horror at New London.

Only when classes resumed and the roll was called on March 29, 1937, could the official death count be confirmed. A total of 280 students and 13 teachers, administrative employees and visitors had lost their lives in the worst school disaster in American history.

Seventy-eight years have come and gone since the unthinkable happened at New London, Texas. Time may have healed the wounds, but not even eternity can erase the scars. There is no way to forget that terrible day the children did not come home from school.

But life goes on, and in East Texas, that meant the wells kept pumping. Many of the thirty thousand are still hard at it to this day. Oil industry estimates put the total production at five and a half *billion* barrels in the eighty-five years since Dad Joiner brought in the Daisy Bradford No. 3.

BIBLIOGRAPHY

Blodgett, Dorothy, Terrell Blodgett and David L. Scott. *The Land, the Law and the Lord: The Life of Pat Neff.* Austin, TX: Home Place Publishers, 2007.

Gould, Lewis L. *Progressives & Prohibitionists: Texas Democrats in the Wilson Era.* Austin: University of Texas Press, 1973.

Handbook of Texas Online. Texas State Historical Association. Austin, TX.

House, Boyce. *Roaring Ranger: The World's Biggest Boom.* San Antonio, TX: Naylor Company, 1951.

———. *Were You in Ranger?* Dallas, TX: Tardy Publishing Company Inc., 1935.

Krenek, Harry. *The Power Vested: The Use of Martial Law and the National Guard in Texas Domestic Crisis 1919–1932.* Austin, TX: Presidial Press, 1980.

Simmons, Nanine. *Booming Mexia in the Roaring 20's.* Waco, TX: Times-Herald, February 9–March 7, 1955.

Sinise, Jerry. *Black Gold & Red Lights.* Fort Worth, TX: Eakin Press, 1982.

Welch, June Rayfield. *The Texas Governor.* Dallas, TX: G.L.A. Press, 1977.

INDEX

INDEX

INDEX

INDEX

Wolters, General Jacob F. 69, 70, 72,
    73, 74, 75, 90, 91, 92, 93, 94,
    106, 108
Womack, Jack 70, 71
World's Richest Acre 105
World War II 101
Wortham, Texas 54, 63
Wyoming 53

Y

Yeti 78
Young Community 73

About the Author

B artee Haile began writing "This Week in Texas History" in 1983 for small-town and suburban newspapers across the Lone Star State. Thirty-two years and more than 1,600 columns later, it is the most widely read and longest-running feature of its kind, ever.

Texas Boomtowns: A History of Blood and Oil is his third book for The History Press. His understanding of the people and places that transformed Texas into the preeminent petroleum power of the twentieth century, along with his entertaining storyteller style, makes it a fascinating page-turner.

A fourth or fifth-generation Texan (he can't really say for sure), Bartee Haile lives in the Houston area with his wife, Gerri.